# The Dirty Thirty

*This book is dedicated to all the members
of the Dirty Thirty and their families, plus
all their supporters throughout the world.
A few names are mentioned in the book,
but there are thousands more. The Dirty
Thirty acknowledge a debt of gratitude to
all of them.*

# The Dirty Thirty

## Heroes of the Miners' Strike

*David Bell*

*David Bell* (signature)

Five Leaves

**The Dirty Thirty**
*by David Bell*

Published in 2009 by Five Leaves,
PO Box 8786, Nottingham NG1 9AW
www.fiveleaves.co.uk

Photographs and images supplied by David Bell
and members of The Dirty Thirty
ISBN: 978 1 905512 67 6

Five Leaves acknowledges financial support
from Arts Council England

Five Leaves is a member of Inpress
(www.inpressbooks.co.uk),
representing independent publishers

Typesetting and design by Four Sheets Design and Print
Printed by the MPG Books Group in the UK

# Contents

# The Dirty Thirty*

Malcolm Pinnegar — "Benny"
Mick Richmond — "Richo"
Mel Elcock
Darren Moore
Dave Douglas
Phil Smith
Cliff Jeffery — "Geek"
Bobby Girvan
Nigel Jeffery
Sammy Girvan
Alan Findell — "Chunk"
Mick Poli
Mark Findell
Ron McKillop
Brian Pallet
Mick Barnes
John Chiswell — "Chiz"

Andrew Warren — "Bunny"
Charlie Burton — "Waggy"
Johnny Gamble
Martin Concannon
Barry Draycott
Keith Mellin
John Shirkie
Bob McSporran
 *(power group president)*
Bobby Howard —
 "Geordie Bob"
Gordon Smith
Gordon Birkin
Billy Scott
Dave Bater
Chris Burford

*Yes, there are 31 names here! The number varied — at one time there were almost 40 (The Naughty Forty?). However the number was never less than 30. They did discover, when they went back, that there was at least one other guy that they had no contact with who hadn't been to work while the strike was on.

7

# Introduction

This book tells the story of thirty men, miners from the Leicestershire coalfield, and the year they voted with their feet to support the miners' strike. Two and a half thousand men in the coalfield continued to work, to cross picket lines, but the Dirty Thirty spent a difficult twelve months on strike, living in a community that disapproved of what they were doing. Some of the disapproval was verbal – abuse in the street, threats on the phone – but occasionally it turned to actual physical violence.

Although their local fellow-miners were against the Dirty Thirty, their own wives and families fully

*Dirty Thirty banner (1984/85).*

supported their action, and they found support from some surprising quarters. Support groups were set up in Leicester, Loughborough, Hinckley and even in Coalville in the heart of the coalfield. Nurses, teachers, engineers, local government staff, all kinds of workers rallied to the cause. In Coalville, local railwaymen – from both the NUR and ASLEF – supported the striking miners. The Dirty Thirty still speak with gratitude and respect about the value of the help they got from the railwaymen of the Mantle Lane depot in Coalville.

Initially, much time was spent in picketing and raising funds. The Dirty Thirty received no money from the National Union of Miners because the local officials were opposed to what they were doing. They also travelled all over the country, to Milton Keynes and Northampton, to South Wales and Scotland, raising funds and spreading the word. One of the Dirty Thirty went on a speaking tour of Umbria, in central Italy. Six of the striking miners were invited to a socialist rally in the USA – at Oberlin College in Ohio – where they rubbed shoulders with the African National Congress from South Africa and the Sandinistas from Nicaragua.

The name *The Dirty Thirty* was originally given to the Leicestershire striking miners by one of their enemies, intended as an insult. But they decided to take it on and wear it as a badge of pride, in the manner of the Old Contemptibles, the members of the British Expeditionary Force insultingly referred to in 1914 by Kaiser Wilhelm II who urged his forces to "walk over that contemptible little army," who decided to wear the insult with pride. Dirty Thirty leader Malcolm Pinnegar – Benny to his friends –

admits that he was doubtful about the name at first. "I didn't think it was a good idea when Richo – Mick Richmond – suggested that we use the name, but I'm very glad we did. Looking back it was a brilliant name, and everyone soon became identified under the Dirty Thirty banner."

Nineteen of the Dirty Thirty came from one pit: Bagworth. The others came from Ellistown and Whitwick, and one brave soul from South Leicester colliery, Johnny Gamble, came out on his own.

*Richo in 1984.*

My own part in the Dirty Thirty story was embarrassingly minor. I attended some meetings of the Coalville support group, and I helped collect food outside a supermarket in Ashby-de-la-Zouch – we had a home-made poster asking shoppers to buy an extra tin of food, and donate it to support the families of the Dirty Thirty. I also collected 50p a week from a number of supporters, a voluntary levy on members of Ashby Labour Party, some £900 in total, and I donated the last eight copies of a children's book I'd written to be sold for the cause.

*Twenty-five years on: Malcolm Pinnegar (Benny) and Richo (Mick Richmond) in 2009.*

10

It was ironic that the Ashby branch was solidly behind the Dirty Thirty, while the Labour Party branches in Coalville, Whitwick, Ellistown – all the mining areas – were not. The reason is simple – their members were working miners. I only met two members of the Dirty Thirty at that time. One was Richo who came to speak to the Coalville Support Group, and the other was Gordon Smith, who came to Ashby to help when we were doing the "buy-an-extra-tin" supermarket appeal. The rest of the Dirty Thirty were just names of people I read about in the local papers, but to me they were heroes, men of principle and courage, ordinary working blokes who knew that what they were doing was the right thing to do.

I must make it plain that the subtitle of this book – *Heroes of the Miners' Strike* – is mine. Benny and the others all deny that they were heroes, but the readers of this book can make up their own minds.

*David Bell*

# Start of the Strike

Margaret Thatcher planned for the 1984-85 miners' strike very carefully. She was very resentful that a miners' strike ten years earlier had brought down a Tory government, when Prime Minister Ted Heath had gone to the country under the slogan, "Who Governs Britain?" and received the dusty answer – Not you! She also had an ideological motive. If she could close down the whole mining industry apart from half a dozen very profitable pits, these could be sold off to private owners. Moreover, if she could defeat the miners' union, widely regarded as the vanguard of the union movement, she would then be able to pick off other unions one by one, and take the country's workers back to the situation before unions began to gain some influence, back to what she regarded as a time when the workers knew their place.

Coal stocks at power stations were built up massively, and the American businessman Ian McGregor

*The Dirty Thirty badge.*

– thought less likely than a Briton to be tainted by the temptation to negotiate and compromise – was appointed as chairman of the Coal Board. Then it was time to provoke the strike she wanted. It was important that it should happen in early spring, because a miners' strike was always

12

more successful during winter months. When the moment arrived, the closure of Cortonwood colliery in South Yorkshire – in the home territory of the NUM president, Arthur Scargill – was designed to be the catalyst for the fight to come. Yorkshire miners came out on strike, as did Scotland, South Wales, Kent, Derbyshire, County Durham and elsewhere.

The strike began for the Leicestershire miners on the evening of Wednesday 14th March 1984, when pickets arrived from the Kent coalfield. According to Sam Girvan, Kent was very much the same kind of coalfield as Leicestershire. "The Kent lads were a bit like us. There were people amongst them who'd originally come down from Durham, Scotland and Wales. Kent was a little island that was going to get shut down totally. You could see a lot of parallels. You could identify with them." One difference however was that Kent had traditionally been a militant area, whereas, in the words of Darren Moore, "the Leicestershire NUM had historically been aligned to Notts and the Spencerites." The Spencer union – the Nottingham and District Miners' Industrial Union – was set up by George Spencer MP following the 1926 strike to cater for those men who wanted to co-operate fully with the mine owners, and to refrain from striking. It was always regarded as a right wing, pro-boss, scab organisation. Although it disappeared with the nationalisation of the pits in 1947, some of its attitudes lingered on in the East Midlands.

Malcolm Pinnegar recalled, "One Wednesday in March 1984, I came up from working on the afternoon shift to find that Bagworth was being picketed

13

by men from Kent." Once Malcolm saw the pickets, he knew that he would not be going to work the next day. Crossing a picket line was completely against his code, and his way of life. He explained, "As I drove out of the pit car park, the Kent pickets were just arriving. I stopped and spoke to them, telling them that I was now on strike and wishing them all the best. I went home and informed my wife that the pickets had arrived and I was now on strike for the duration."

Mel Elcock felt the same. "My family had a history of fighting the enemies of this country in wartime and also the enemies of the union in peacetime, so you can see what sort of stock I come from. We don't run away from a fight. If it's there and we feel that it's our fight, then we'll make a stand. We'll not shy away from it. And it was right, and it's been proved right.

"Prior to the 84 strike, everyone knew it was coming. Everybody was talking about it. There were a lot of Scotsmen and a lot of Geordies working in the pit. We'd sit talking about it and you would have thought by what I was hearing that there wouldn't have been two ways about it, Bagworth would have gone on strike. There were some talking against it, but in the main people seemed to be in favour of defending their industry. When the Kent pickets first came, I just turned round and went home, and I thought everybody would do the same. We'd been picketed out and nobody should cross a picket line. It was a long-standing thing: miners do not cross a picket line. Then it was on the news that the pit was working normally. Well, I knew I wasn't the only one who'd gone home. A lot more than thirty went home at that time. Well I turned back the next day and the pickets spoke to us. They said the best thing to do was to go in and try and organise from inside the pit, try and get more support. So that's what we decided to do."

Malcolm, Richo and Phil Smith were also among those strikers asked by the pickets to go back to work for a week or so, to try to persuade the working miners to come out, but they found that most refused to join the strike. Malcolm tells me that he came out of work an hour early on the day the pickets arrived because he'd been working in water all shift and the deputy had given him an early exit paper. This made him the first man in Leicestershire to be on strike. Darren Moore was on a City and Guilds mining apprenticeship, training to be a deputy or a foreman. He went down the pit, taking turns at doing all different jobs and went to Coalville Tech one day per week. He told me, "When the strike started, I'd done all the training apart from shot firing, and in fact, when the Kent miners came up to picket at the start of the strike, I was at tech that day so I didn't see any of that happen. I was a bit left wing, and I'd got the view that I would be on strike to save jobs and to prevent the Tories decimating the unions. I was anticipating that we would all be out, although I had no faith in the local NUM leadership at the time, Jack Jones and Trevor Hines particularly."

One Leicestershire miner who knew the Kent pickers were coming was Keith Mellin, who was working at Ellistown pit. Keith had been a Kent miner himself, but had moved to Leicestershire in 1981, when he married a Leicestershire girl. He told me, "Before the Kent pickets came up, I got a phone call from some of the lads who I'd worked with, asking me what was going on. I couldn't tell them a lot, to be honest, because there was nothing going on. I couldn't understand the lack of response from the whole area. I think the lack of response was the biggest shock to people from outside the area. I thought it would get a far better response than it did. If it had split 80%-20% even, there'd have been five hundred of us out. I don't know what the percentage is for thirty of us but it's not much more than 1%. I knew quite a few of the Kent lads who came up to picket, and they came to my house. I'd decided I was going to strike a long time before, regardless of the local leaders."

The day after the Kent pickets arrived, Thursday 15th March, they were allowed to address a meeting of Bagworth miners in the canteen, and the men present decided to come out and support the strike. Darren's diary for that day reads: "At the meeting in the canteen, all eighty men decided to strike and to picket. Trevor Hines, our union delegate at Bagworth, was supposed to go and tell the other pits we were out, to urge them to support us, but instead he had gone off to Bakewell Street in Coalville, to see Jack Jones, the area NUM secretary, who came in and told the men to go back to work, saying the strike was unconstitutional." Jack Jones and the other union right-wingers came up with a delaying tactic to prevent any pro-strike momentum building up, demanding a local ballot before striking. With most of the Leicestershire pits running out of coal and due to close, the local ballot went against the strike.

Mel Elcock had a similar experience of being at a meeting where the vote was to support the strike, only to find that the local union leadership had sabotaged the decision. "We were the power group, fitters and electricians, and we had a meeting in the workshop. Bob McSporran, who was the NUM Power Group area president, addressed the meeting, and it was practically unanimous to go on strike. I know a lot of lads who then went straight out and formed a picket line, and encouraged people not to work. At the end of that day I went home and it come on the radio that Bagworth was working normally. I rang the union office, not really expecting anyone to be there, and our delegate, Pat Callaghan, picked the phone up. I asked him, 'What's happening, because I've just heard that pit was working normally, yet I'm at home on strike. We voted.' He said, 'Oh, we had another vote when the afternoon shift come in.' I told him, 'You can't keep voting until you get the vote that you want. It's going to go on forever. You're making yourself look silly and you're making Leicestershire miners look silly, as well.' Unfortunately the decision was made then. The people that went to work went to work and the people that stayed out on strike stayed out. There was four of us from Bagworth power group who went on strike: Andy Warren, John Chiswell, Mark Findell and me."

Once it became clear that the majority of miners were not going to join the strike, Richo felt bad at being down the pit at all, even though the pickets had asked them to. "By the end of the second week, I was going mental, because it was wrong, what we were doing. I was crossing a picket line, and I just couldn't do it. And that was that." Malcolm, Richo, Mel and the others came out of the pit and rejoined the picket line. By now the Kent pickets had moved on, and had been replaced by pickets from South Wales.

Andy Warren told me, "I was the same as everybody else and knew a strike was coming sooner or later. Whether it was right or wrong, there was no way I could cross a picket line so the first day the pickets arrived that was it. I was out on strike. There was hundreds of good union men who were mixed up and told by local union officials to work until we had a ballot, some thinking they might get a few extra shifts in before they were called out on strike. Local union officials decided to try and keep everybody at work and some good union men were misled by these officials. Some who didn't believe in striking used these officials as an excuse to carry on working, persuading others it was the right thing to do. After a few weeks, those who were conned into staying at work were used to crossing picket lines and for whatever reason carried on working, leaving people such as myself deemed on strike."

More of the Dirty Thirty came out soon afterwards. Cliff Jeffery – Geek – told me, "If my memory serves me correct, it was three weeks into the strike when I decided to join the strikers. Previously it had been galling to me, passing the pickets every day. These guys were trying to save our jobs and we were going to work. Down the pit at that time, most of the talk was about the strike and I frequently heard the phrase, 'We should be with them,' but nobody put their money where their mouth was, so to speak. Well finally I'd had enough so out I came. Ever since

I started work at Nailstone Colliery in 1950, I had always been a great believer in the union, although never an active member. I had already been through two strikes so this was my third, and although Scargill refused to have a ballot – which was his mistake because he would have got an overwhelming yes, in my opinion – I believed we should unite and stand as one. The result could have been a lot different if every miner had come out." At the Jeffery household, it was not just Cliff who came out. His son Nigel and his two stepsons, Alan and Mark Findell, also joined the strike. Geek was one of the most respected of the Dirty Thirty; and everyone told me what a great bloke he was. Sam Girvan said, "I'd say Cliff was the most respected man at Bagworth. He'd treat everybody the same. 'We'll have a minute, Old Crust,' he used to say." Sam's brother Bob added, "He had credibility. People could say, 'Oh, the Girvans would be on strike anyway, they wouldn't need an excuse,' but when Cliff came out, the number one lamp-holder, they had to think again."

Cliff's view that there should have been a national ballot on the strike is a minority one within the Dirty Thirty. I believe that Mel Elcock speaks for the majority when he explained that the idea of the national ballot had been killed off a few years earlier by a decision of a judge, who ruled that local areas could ignore the national result if they wished. "The national ballot was killed in 1976, when there was a national ballot on the bonus scheme. Until then, everybody believed in the national ballot." The NUM nationally was opposed to the bonus scheme on the grounds of safety and because it would set area against area, pit against pit. Mel continued, "We got a national vote in 1976 on the bonus scheme, but Leicestershire, Nottinghamshire and South Derbyshire reneged on the ballot. That was the end of the national ballot idea. Yorkshire miners, Welsh miners, Kent miners, miners in the North-East were all saying, 'You're not stabbing us in the back with a national ballot again. We know what you want to do. If we have a ballot and it goes for a strike we know what you'll do, you'll carry on working.' A national ballot wouldn't have made any difference; that was proved in 1976. We knew the Leicestershire NUM leadership would not abide by the result of a national ballot if it went against them."

Keith Mellin agreed, saying, "Now, if there'd have been a vote, and at the time it would have probably been a national majority to strike, after a couple of months there'd have been arguments that certain areas had voted against the strike and they should be allowed to go to work."

The Dirty Thirty now knew that the local NUM leadership was vehemently opposed to them and to the strike. Mel Elcock argued, "Unfortunately the leadership in Leicestershire has always been very weak. Jack Jones was the leader at the time, and basically he was encouraging all the people to go to work. He was even saying that if necessary he would lead them into work carrying a baseball bat. It was in the newspapers at the time." Darren Moore's comment was, "I felt very demoralised and disappointed that Leicestershire miners were giving me stick and crossing picket lines now that the local NUM had endorsed this course of action. The pickets from South Wales could not understand why the men were crossing the picket line because their tradition was that if there's a picket line you don't cross it."

Two or three of the Dirty Thirty – Nigel Jeffery, Sam Girvan, Johnny Gamble – were on the sick when the strike began. Sam had quite a problem getting the management to realise he was on strike. "Just before the strike, I got buried underneath some coal. A prop hit me, knocked me onto the ground, and then what's called a raker came down and hit me as well, but luckily the raker stopped the rest coming on me. I got carried out the pit, had a check-up in the hospital, then I was on the sick with a bad back. I was told that I couldn't go on strike while I was on the sick – and that was from a union man at the time, Trevor Hines. In March, I sat there and I said, 'Well, I've got to go back to work just to be on strike!' My principles were saying I was getting something for nothing on the sick when there were other people on strike. Being a socialist, if you like, I didn't think it was right even to be on the sick when people were on strike. So I went back to work, went in and said to the union, 'I want to be on strike.' They said, 'You can't be on strike while you're on the sick.' I was about 24 or 25, young family and that. My wife knew when I sat watching them, when the pickets were coming, there was no way I would cross the picket line. I went down the pit for one day, came straight out that night, on strike. I stood talking to the pickets, and they said, 'If you turn up tomorrow, you can join the picket line.' Again the union man came and said, 'You can't go on strike, because Leicestershire's not on strike.' I said, 'Well, *I'm* on strike.' There was a vote but it wasn't really a proper vote. Let's just put it this way, it went the way the Leicestershire union officials wanted it to."

Johnny Gamble, who worked at South colliery, told me that like Sam Girvan he was off work when the strike began. "I'd been on the club for six weeks, as I'd broken my finger. I don't know if it was the Tuesday or the Wednesday when it all kicked off, but that was my last week on the club. Then on the Monday I went to work, went through the picket line, and sat in the canteen listening to blokes coming out with 'They'll never get us on strike,' and all that crap. I knew I wasn't where I wanted to be. I actually went down the pit, went into the district and what I heard all day was men saying that they were never going on strike, and I thought, 'Well, I am.' So I actually went out the pit and saw the union man. Luckily for me,

I'd probably got the most sympathetic union man in Leicestershire, Terry Tracey. I think all my lodge members would have liked to have been on strike, but because the area didn't want to go on strike, they couldn't. Technically they couldn't." After talking to Terry, Johnny came out and became the only man at South pit to join the strike. No-one could disagree with Sam Girvan when he commented, "It was very courageous of Johnny to be the only man in South out." Actually there may have been a second man from South on strike. Gordon Smith, who joined the Dirty Thirty, tells me that although he went to his place of work underground via the drift at Snibston, he actually was paid from South, and used the baths there.

Dave Douglas was another miner who had definite views about crossing a picket line. "Whenever there was a picket there, I weren't crossing it. Whether there was one man there or a hundred men, I wasn't going to cross it. Whatever the vote in Leicestershire, I wasn't going to cross a picket line. It was a shock to see how many actually did. When you sat talking to them down the pit, they said, 'Oh, I'd never cross a picket line.' These were people who'd come from Scotland, Yorkshire, men that you wouldn't expect to cross. I remember the Kent lads being there on the Friday. I went to the pit, saw the Kent lads and turned round and went back. My wife Kath was heavily pregnant at the time. She was due to have our first child, my son. This would be the 30th March. On that Friday, I didn't cross the picket line. On the Saturday, Kath's waters broke and she had the baby on the Monday morning, 2nd April. Then I never even went to the pit for a week, I had a week off, not doing anything. I turned up a week later, and the pickets were there. I never spoke to anybody, just turned round and went home. I did that for about three weeks. But I never saw anybody's face on the picket line that I knew, to stop and talk to. I didn't see Benny or any of them. I didn't see any of the lads that I found out later were on strike. At the time, I didn't know who were on strike from Leicester. I didn't know whether I was on my own."

Bobby Girvan and Mick Barnes were two more who thought they might be the only people who were on strike. Bobby told me, "After speaking to the pickets a few times, I'd go down and I'd argue and argue, trying to tell the men we should be out. And to be fair, there were people – people who didn't strike – who were saying we *should* all be out. But the leadership from the local union wasn't there. Then it came to a bit of a crunch time after about a month, and I wasn't comfortable about going down at all, and Mick Barnes come round. He said, 'Me and you'll start a picket line Bobby.' Mick talks with a Bristol twang. They nicknamed him Jesus because he looked like a hippy. I said, 'Well it's going to look bad, Mick. We'll look like Wolfie and Tucker off of Citizen Smith.' At the time, I thought we might be the only ones out."

There were other men out on strike, but no-one knew who they were or how many there were. It was time for a bit of leadership, a bit of organisation.

# The Dirty Thirty Organise

One problem faced by the striking miners was that they did not live in a compact community. As Bob Girvan told me, "You've got to remember that we were living in an area forty mile wide." Mel Elcock lived in Loughborough, Dave Douglas and Barry Draycott lived in Leicester, Malcolm Pinnegar in Stoney Stanton, a village some fifteen miles south of Coalville. Obviously some of them knew each other – Bob and Sam Girvan were brothers, Nigel and Cliff Jeffery, Mark and Andrew Findell were from the same household. But there were four pits, Bagworth, Whitwick, Ellistown and South, and miners from one pit didn't really know the miners from the others. Even miners from the same pit might only be on nodding terms, "ey-up" terms, with one another but not much more than passing acquaintances.

Dave Douglas told me, "I never worked with Benny or any of them. I'd met Darren a few times down the pit, because he was moving around, doing different jobs. I knew the Girvans, Bobby and Sammy, and I'd met Geek. When you'd done your initial six months face training, you become what they call a market lad, a spare, filling in anywhere if someone's not turned in, until a job becomes available, and obviously I'd met Geek on that. And Richo used to run the main gate supply on my dad's face, so through that I'd got to know Richo quite well, even before the strike. I knew Benny by sight but I'd never had much to do with him."

Darren Moore reminisced, "We decided we needed to organise, as the strike was starting to go on for some time and people were struggling for money. We met in the Barrel pub up the road in Bagworth to decide how to organise, as it was looking like others would not come out and we could not cross picket lines. The meeting at the Barrel was our first real meeting where we decided what we were going to do, how we were going to sort ourselves out. It was easy for me in a lot of respects because I was single, I was living at home at the time, I'd got no children, so I hadn't got any massive responsibilities. I said that for my part, I was happy to do picketing and fundraising anywhere, go and collect money to make sure I could help people stay out on strike. That was my contribution as it had been got to a point where after weeks and weeks, there was no money coming in, and people were saying, 'I'm struggling. I want to stay out but I've got no money,' so we needed to sort all that out. By this stage it was clear that only a mass picket would stop people returning to work so I thought fundraising was a priority to make sure we were able to stay out and spread the message that the Tories were out to break the working class."

At the meeting, Malcolm was elected as leader, as he had experience of a long strike at Imperial Typewriters when he was working there. Richo was to be his co-leader, in charge of organising the pickets, and in charge of the group's publicity. Ron McKillop was elected as treasurer. Mel Elcock and Darren Moore also volunteered to be part of the organising committee. Richo commented, "Obviously Benny was the right man for the job of leader, because he knew about trade unions." Malcolm returned the compliment saying, "Having Richo as co-leader did turn out to be brilliant, because of what he done. It's because of Richo that we became better known. It massively raised the profile of the Dirty Thirty and also helped us raise money."

Dave Douglas, who lived in Leicester, hadn't heard about the early meetings. "I didn't know whether I was out on my own. After three or four weeks, I thought I'd better go and find out what was happening. I ought to go in and talk to the lads. I got to the picket line and the only face I knew was a chap called Mick Barnes, who was on strike. He says, 'Ah Dave, we've been looking for you. We understood you were out but nobody knew where you lived.' Living in Leicester I was out the way of everybody. He says, 'Give us your phone number and we'll give you a ring.' I went back home again, and I got a ring. 'Meet us tomorrow at the Spread Eagle in Leicester.' So I went down Leicester and met all the lads there. It was, 'Where've you been?' 'I've been at home. I kept going to the pit, seeing the picket line and I wouldn't cross it and I'd go back home. I didn't know who was out and who wasn't.'"

Most of the organising at the early meetings was by the miners from Bagworth pit. Because he was from Ellistown pit, Keith Mellin felt even more out of things. "At Ellistown, there was just me, Martin Concannon, Barry Draycott, John Shirkie, and Bob MacSporran out. We didn't know about the Bagworth men for weeks and weeks. It was like no contact between us. I was living in Whitwick and it was all very isolated. I kept in touch with Martin, to see what was going on. It was about six weeks before I heard anything about the other miners who were on strike. They made contact, and told us there were about twenty out from Bagworth, and that Benny, Richo, Mel, and Ronny McKillop were getting organised. They were the main organisers. Me and Martin tended to stick with Mel and Ronny, doing stuff. Collecting food, the mundane stuff. Trying to drum up support, going to meetings, Labour groups and things like that."

Other jobs were sorted out at the early meetings of the Dirty Thirty. Phil Smith volunteered to run the food collections, sorting the donated food into thirty bags and delivering them to the families every week. "My garage was like Asda. I'd got my little Renault Five. I used to go to the supermarket, buy something small, and grab a handful of plastic bags, then I used them to bag all the food up. Martin and Keith, they used to get the bacon, and cheese. Everybody used to get a packet of cheese and bacon every week. I used to take it in my car, when we had the meeting every Friday. Put the flap down, put in the thirty bags or whatever it was. I used to be fair. Nobody got any more than anybody else, including the single lads. It wasn't just for the ones with families. If the single lads gave it to one of the other families, that was up to them."

When Leicester City Council let the Dirty Thirty have an office at a peppercorn rent of £1 a week, it was natural that Dave Douglas, living in Leicester, should be the one to open it up every morning.

"Eventually we got the Miners' Strike Centre in a municipal building in Charles Street, above Willy Thorne's snooker place. That became our centre post of Leicester. Everything that was happening in Leicester went through that office. I can't remember whether I volunteered or if it just happened, but I went in every day. I opened it up in the morning at nine o'clock and I was there until I knew nobody else was coming in. There were no set times. Mainly people from the support group were coming in every day. Kay Smith came in now and again. Anybody who was coming to Leicester would come in. It was our focal point."

Phil Smith also used to help at the Leicester office. "I used to do the office as well. Dave and me, we used to do that between us. Dave lived in Leicester, so he'd open it up and I'd go up about dinner time." Supporters would also call into the Charles Street office to talk to the miners, to bring in donated food, to bring in money. Malcolm Pinnegar mentioned to me an occasion when a lady came into the Dirty Thirty's Leicester office. She explained that her elderly father had just died and left her a few hundred pounds, which she was donating to the cause. The strikers were very reluctant to take her money but she insisted, saying that her dad had been in the 1926 General Strike and would want them to have it.

Richo tells me about a significant event that occurred when his wife Linda tried to ring him at the Leicester strike office, only to have the phone answered by an officer at Syston Police Station. It soon became obvious that the strike office phone was being tapped, as were the phones of many of the Dirty Thirty members. On one occasion Richo and Malcolm decided to test this theory. Richo said, "Me and Benny, we always knew that our phones were tapped. You could hear it. I said to Benny, 'There's only me and you going to know about this. I'm going to phone you later on, about seven o'clock, and I'm going to tell you that the North Derbyshire pickets are coming down and they're coming to Whitwick pit. But they're not. We'll just see what happens.' I phoned him and gave him that message, and then I walked down Whitwick Road. You've never seen anything like it. It was completely blocked with police cars and vans. I went to a public phone box and I phoned Benny, and I says, 'I wish you were here. It's worked. The road outside Whitwick pit is full of police.' So that proved it conclusively. The government seemed to have limitless powers at their disposal, and money was no object. When the national NUM ran short of money in their strike fund and began to use money from their much larger general funds to help the families of the striking miners, it was the courts that decided this was illegal and sequestrated the union funds. The police seemed to abandon any attempt to be neutral during the strike and became, in many eyes, a partisan force at the disposal of the state. In his excellent book, *The Enemy Within* – not to be confused with a book with a similar title written by Ian McGregor – Seumas Milne provided convincing evidence of the secret role played by MI5 as they worked to undermine the national strike leaders. Milne provides compelling evidence that, using phoney bank deposits, staged cash drops, forged documents, agents provocateurs and unrelenting surveillance, MI5 set out to discredit Arthur Scargill and the other miners' leaders. It is today accepted by most commentators that they also had a mole within the NUM national office. Money to defeat the strike was no problem to the government, and six million pounds was spent to police Leicestershire alone where just thirty men were on strike.

As the strike continued, the Dirty Thirty continued to meet once a week, sorting out the picketing rota, deciding what would happen during the next week, who would be doing what. Occasionally, some of the rank and file didn't appreciate the tight discipline. Bob and Sam Girvan told me, "There was Richo and Benny, Mel Elcock, Ronny McKillop, Darren Moore, they were the main five of them. We used to go and listen to our instructions, then go ahead and do our own thing. And even a few years after the strike, nobody realised how much work other people did. A lot of people put in a lot of hard work."

Dave Douglas summed up the situation very well when he explained, "We were thirty strong characters. Of course there were tensions, there were bound to be." Nigel Jeffery commented, "In our situation we needed strong leaders."

What was important was not the differences between the members of the Dirty Thirty, but what they had in common.

# Support for the Thirty

Everyone in the Dirty Thirty tells me how grateful they were for the support they got from the railwaymen who worked at Mantle Lane in Coalville. The Coalville railworkers decided to back the Dirty Thirty by blacking the movement of coal by rail, and eventually persuaded the national leadership of their unions – the NUR and ASLEF – to back them. Bob Girvan said, "We've got to remember the people round Coalville who put their jobs on the line for us, like the railwaymen. They were fantastic." Nigel Jeffery told me, "The railwaymen gave us great support." Malcolm Pinnegar commented, "The railwaymen – especially at the Coalville depot – were terrific. Many of them refused to handle coal trucks, and, like us, they had to live in an area where the consensus was against them."

Mick Richmond had more memories about the Mantle Lane men. "Round here in Coalville, the railwaymen were heroes, they really were. Absolute heroes. I remember little Ernie Hallam, bless him, he was a signalman, he's got one leg shorter than the other, got a special boot made. Brilliant guy. Out and out socialist. And he would not signal coal. He was based at Bardon, on the signal box there. I used to go up and sit with him. I'd say, 'When's the next train coming?' and he'd say, 'Any minute, but it won't get past.' And it didn't. It would sit there until he finished his shift, and then one of his colleagues would come on, what we called scabs, and he'd signal it through. They stopped a lot of coal going through, the local railwaymen. I don't know how many millions of tons it was, but they were fantastic. Roy Butlin, Graham Cross, Dennis Wright, Phil Davies, Roy 'Taggart' Clark, loads of them. Fantastic people." Roy Butlin was the NUR leader in Coalville, and a man whom the Dirty Thirty regard with tremendous affection and respect for the support he gave them, putting his own job prospects at risk to fight the same struggle as the local striking miners.

Anthony Gregory was a trainee driver and an ASLEF member, also based at Coalville. He writes, "Coalville depot was soon in the thick of it. As we talked it over with my colleagues, it was soon clear that we were in support of the strike and greatly admired the striking miners and their families. Men

*The railwaymen unite with the Dirty Thirty.*
*Back l to r: Two railwaymen, Nigel Jeffery, Richo.*
*Front: Gordon Smith, Bobby Girvan, Geordie Bob, Brian Pallet,*
*Phil Smith.*

*Joint poster of Mantle Lane railwaymen and the Dirty Thirty.*

at our depot knew as far back as 1983 that something was brewing. We couldn't stock up the power stations quickly enough. As space ran out at one Midlands power station, the perimeter access road was covered in thousands of tons of coal. It seemed as if a plan was being prepared – a plan for confrontation.

"In April 1984, the first railwaymen were sent home for refusing or blacking the coal. Some of them would not move a coal train for the rest of the year-long dispute. Donations were used to pay train crews for loss of earnings when they were sent home, as British Rail would not pay for refusal to work. When I returned to the Colville depot from my six-month's driver training in Derby, I was asked to second man a coal train. I refused and was sent home. This became a regular occurrence. On nights, we were regularly stopped by police looking for flying pickets. When I told them I worked at Coalville, some got quite obnoxious with me. Coalville depot was well known for its support of the miners. A local Tory MP even publicly accused one signalman of being mentally unstable for refusing to pull off his signals.

"In the Coalville area, a small group of miners, known as the Dirty Thirty, stayed out for the duration. They had to put up with considerable violence and abuse from working miners. They sometimes came to meetings or down to the depot and they were given a warm welcome by most blokes. Later in the year, railwaymen from Coalville were invited to Kersley Colliery Miners Club in Coventry. We filled a 52 seater bus, and were present to see the unveiling of a railwayman shaking hands with a miner. When we were called up onto the stage we were given a standing ovation. The whole event was charged with emotion."

The standing ovation for the railwaymen of Coalville was richly deserved. Like the Dirty Thirty, they lived among communities of working miners, and had to put up with disapproval and abuse for their courageous stand. It is no wonder that the Dirty Thirty regard them as heroes.

More backing for the Thirty came from local support groups. The Leicester Support Group was the first in the country to be set up, established even before there was a Dirty Thirty to support. Its chair was Mick Jarmaine and its secretary was a nurse from Leicester Royal Infirmary, Jane Bruton. Other names warmly remembered by members of the Dirty Thirty include Melvyn Pack, Paul Mason, Tony Stephens, Paul Winston, Colin Green, Betty Shields, Tony Baron and Dave Bent of the Leicester Unemployed Centre, Bob Waterton, Paul Gosling, Jim Doohar and Karen Whitelaw.

Malcolm Pinnegar told me, "A massive thing to us was Leicester Trades Council which formed the Leicester Miners Support Group. The first person we went to see was Jane Bruton, who was a nurse at Leicester Royal. I went to see a steward at the Royal, named Charlie Sorell, and he fetched Jane out. The

Leicester Support Group made our job a million times easier. Leicester University was very active in our support. The student union was brilliant; we were made honorary members for life. Probably the hardest speaking job I ever did was one dinner time, when I had to speak in front of all the students. They raised thousands of pounds for us. We were barracked by some white coated Tory students who tried to heckle us. They didn't do very well because the other students shouted them down. The lecturers at the University and what was then the Leicester Poly paid levies out of their pay all through the strike for us. Everybody who was into leftist politics was our supporter, including Leicester City Council. They let us have a strike office for just £1 a week, and they did take some stick for it from the local Tories. We appreciate that for them it was a big risk."

One memorable event put on by the Leicester Support Group was a play *With the Sun On Our Backs,* performed by Utility Theatre Company, a co-

operative theatre group working mainly in the East Midlands. The company was founded by Timothy Poole, and I note from the play programme that he played six parts: Al, Bill, police officer, second police officer, Italian man and TV repair man! The play was based on the story of the Dirty Thirty and their families. It was written by Tony

Stephens with music by Paul Mason, both local lecturers. (Paul, incidentally can frequently be seen today on BBC2 *Newsnight*, where he is the economics editor.) The main character is a young woman called Cath, and everyone who has seen the play tells me that it is unmistakably based on Kay Smith, the leader of the Dirty Thirty wives' support group. Phil Smith confirmed this when he told me that Amanda Wyatt, the actress playing Cath, came round to the Smith house in Barlestone on several occasions to study how Kay spoke, to imitate her northwest Leicestershire accent and her speech patterns. As well as its debut at the Haymarket Theatre in Leicester, *With the Sun On Our Backs* was later performed in Coalville, London, Edinburgh and even in Australia.

The Leicester Support Group put on many functions in aid of the Dirty Thirty. At one, hosted by Leicester CND, Bob Girvan decided to perform one of his poems. He recalled, "It was a CND do held at the de Montfort Hall. Some of them were saying, 'What's the miners got to do with this?' This poet gets up – he was quite famous but I can't remember his name – and I thought I could do as well as that. I'd been writing poetry about the strike, so I gets up and starts talking about the miners and it went very quiet. I did one poem, and there was silence. I said, 'Well, that went down a bomb, didn't it?' I got roars of laughter, and then after the next poem – it was about being at Greenham Common, with the women – I got a standing ovation. I was really proud of that."

Both the Girvan brothers are great humorists, and Sam told me that at another do in Leicester, the food was a curry supplied by Indian supporters. All of the

Dirty Thirty mentioned the wonderful support given to them by the Asian communities in Leicester, especially the Indian Workers Association. Sam and Bob decided to try the curry. "They'd got this big pot, massive, with lamb chops and bones and everything. One or two said, 'Come and have a curry.' I was just talking away, and I was eating this curry. It was like fire. Benny was standing there with his daughter, and he said to me, 'Where are you going?' I said, 'I'm going to that window to lick the condensation off it.' My mouth was that hot."

There was also a support group in Loughborough. One of the most active members of the Loughborough support group was Barry Elcock, brother of Mel, a Leicestershire striking miner. Barry told me, "When my brother first went on strike, there was no support group. I went with my brother and Ron McKillop to meet the Loughborough Trades Council, and it was from there that the Loughborough Support Group started. The day we turned up, some Yorkshire miners from Cortonwood – where the strike started – came to try to get the Trades Council to support them. I said, 'Now hold on a minute, there are people here, in our own area, on strike. Before you think about supporting anybody else, you want to talk to these lads.' The Trades Council weren't aware that any Leicestershire miners were on strike. The Yorkshire lads, Mick Carter and Mick Clark, said, 'Yes, that's quite right. You must support your own lads.'

"Mac McLoughlin, the secretary of the Trades Council, became the chair of the Support Group. Also involved there were Russ Bowman, Ray Sutton, Mike Shuker and Geoff Gay. I was an ordinary supporter. I organised a weekly collection at Brush Engineering, where I worked, from as many sympathisers as I could. I'd started that even before the Loughborough Support Group got active. One bloke, Rod, had a brother who was an actual scab miner but Rod was still donating every week to this fund for the Leicestershire striking miners. There was a hardcore who donated every week at the Brush, through the whole of the strike. Where I worked at the Brush, I'd got this corner where I kept all my tools, and I'd got all these big photographs taken out the paper. We blew them up to be about three foot, the posters, especially the Orgreave one. I had them all up, pinned to my wall. When the managing director used to come round, he used to say, 'And here we are in Red Corner.'

"My function in the support group was as the chief fund-raiser. I used to organise discos. I'd try to get people to donate the room, and to donate the bar. Then I'd sell the tickets. I'd find DJs who were union men, and ask them to do it at cost, as cheap as they could. Everything that I raised from that I put into the fund for the Leicestershire Dirty Thirty. But outside of that, I used to go with my brother onto the picket lines. I also used to go to other coalfields – North Derbyshire, Yorkshire – to take surplus food, because we did very well with the food collecting. I've stood outside supermarkets on Christmas Eve, I organised functions, organised people from other areas to come in. To collect the food, we organised two shifts. Somebody would go round putting leaflets through letterboxes, then somebody would follow it up later collecting the food. Ray Sutton used to plot the routes for that, what areas on what days, so we didn't go to the same places too often. It was quite difficult round here because the people of Loughborough couldn't really relate to coalmining. Even though the coalmines were only a few miles up the road, there weren't a lot of miners in Loughborough.

"I suggested at one of the Support Group meetings that we went and stood outside supermarkets, and at first they were saying, 'Oh no, that won't be successful.' I said, 'Let's give it a try.' We went the two weekends before Christmas, when people are prepared to be more generous, and on the actual Christmas weekend. I used to do my shopping at Safeways, so I asked the manager if it would be all right to come out here to collect. He said yes, but the first Saturday we turned up, the police came, saying we had no right to be there and we'd got to move. I told them that the manager had given us permission and they went back in to have a word with him. When they came back they said, 'No, he hasn't given you permission.' Well, that was a lie, he did. But we had to move. We went down to the town to Somerfield supermarket, and they made us welcome. We collected there, the following two weekends. We did well there. We also had people come from other shops, shop owners, giving us stuff. An Irish woman, who was the owner of the café round the corner, the Coffee Pot, she could see we were cold so she came out with a tray of hot coffee for us. She said, 'I know what it's like to struggle. The miners have my sympathy. At the end of today when we shut down for Christmas, I'll bring you a load of food.' Which she did.

"We got Tony Benn to come and speak to a meeting at the Town Hall, which was a resounding

*Tony Benn meets the Dirty Thirty in Loughborough.*
*Ronny McKillop, Nigel Jeffery, Tony Benn, Mel Elcock and*
*Gordon Smith.*

success. When I turned up, the queue to get in was stretching right back down the market. As Town Hall filled up, it was packed to capacity, and everybody was standing at the back of the hall. They had to open the upstairs, and even that was packed. It must have been one of the biggest nights they'd ever had. A very, very successful meeting. Mick Carter from Cortonwood spoke, as did Bob McSporran and Mike McLoughlin. Tony Benn was outstanding. I bet he spoke for a good hour. He really captivated his audience, and you could have heard a pin drop. That's the respect he commanded. A massive amount of money was collected. It was mostly word of mouth that had spread the word. The audience were ordinary factory workers, but when they knew Tony Benn was coming, they all turned out."

Tony Benn has sent me some extracts from his diaries, which he has generously allowed me to quote.

His entry for 13th September 1984 reads: "I was taken to Loughborough for a public meeting organised by the Miners Support Group. It was interesting. There are only thirty miners out of over two thousand in the whole of Leicestershire who are on strike and they had organised the meeting against the opposition of the local Labour Party who said, 'First you'll never get Tony Benn and secondly, you'll only get 100 people and it'll expose our weakness.' In the event, there were 700 in the Town Hall and the collection raised nearly £1200. It was an absolutely fantastic meeting, and they said there hadn't been a socialist meeting like that in Loughborough since the war."

Barry continued, "Just after the strike we had another meeting, and we had Dennis Skinner to speak. That was another success, but it wasn't as big as the Town Hall meeting. We held that meeting at the Bull's Head. The Labour Party members that attended asked me, 'How did you get him? We can't get him.' They didn't really believe we'd got him, so when they turned up they were gobsmacked. This was a function to raise money for the sacked miners." Barry carried on arranging functions for ten years after the strike, raising money for the sacked miners in other coalfields, and in total raised almost two thousand pounds.

There was another Support Group set up in Hinckley and Bosworth, led by Pauline Cuttress. Malcolm tells me that they were his local support group and that he owes them a special thank you, as, because of his other commitments he was unable to give them the assistance they deserved.

There was even a support group in Coalville, in the heart of the coalfield. Apart from Ross Willmott and

Dave Cross, most of its members were from Ashby-de-la-Zouch Labour Party. The reason for this was evident. Labour Party branches in Coalville, Bagworth, Ellistown and elsewhere had members that were working miners, and they disapproved of the Dirty Thirty. Ashby, perhaps regarded as a middle-class branch in Labour Party circles, provided most of the supporters of the strike. These included Peter and Marie Thompson, Clare Fordham and Hamish Rhind, Harriet Foot, Vic O'Brien and others.

Clare and Hamish managed to get themselves arrested on one picket line, where they had gone along to support the strikers. Ordered by the police to move to the far side of the road, to get further away from the miners going to work, Clare asked, 'Why?' She won't thank me for saying so, but Clare has a voice that can only be described as posh. As soon as the police heard the question, Clare was hauled off to the police station. Hamish, by then her partner, tried to hold onto her, and he too was taken away. Clare and Hamish, like Pete and Marie, frequently had visiting pickets from Wales or from Durham sleeping at their house. For Pete Thompson, his support was a typically courageous move, as he was a member of BACM (the coal industry managers' union) and worked at Coleorton Hall, the Coal Board area head-quarters. The Ashby supporters, like those from Loughborough and Leicester, held food collections outside the local supermarket, asking shoppers to buy an extra tin and donate it for the families of the Dirty Thirty. I remember on one occasion, we were approached by a policewoman, and I assumed she had come to move us on. I was wrong; she nodded, smiled and quietly put a fiver into the box.

One local supporter, though not a member of any support group, was the late Eddy Bonner. Malcolm told me, "The most support that we could ever have asked for, all our lads and all the pickets, was from a bloke called Eddy Bonner, who lived opposite the pit at Bagworth. He'd put pickets up in his house, he was fantastic. He was an ex-miner, but he would definitely have been striking."

There was one happy result of the miners' strike and the attendance at a meeting by a female member of "the hard left in Leicester" – her own phrase. Simone Dawes, later to become a member of the Socialist Workers Party, went to a union meeting where a member of the Dirty Thirty, Darren Moore, was speaking. She and the friend who was sitting with her decided that Darren was "a bit of all right." They even joked about whether he was a "horizontal recruiter." At that time Simone was living with someone, but after the strike Simone had "ditched her useless boyfriend," and when she kept seeing Darren at various meetings, she decided to chat him up. They became an item and later married. Darren and Simone have been together ever since, and it was all due to the miners' strike. It was one very good outcome to emerge from the year of the strike.

# The Women's Support Group

One thing that enabled the Dirty Thirty to carry on for a full twelve months was the support of their womenfolk. Their wives, their girlfriends, their mothers, all threw themselves into supporting the strike, raising money, collecting and distributing food donations, accompanying their men on demonstrations and in at least one case, going onto the picket line.

The first meeting of the Dirty Thirty Wives Support Group took place in April 1984 at the home of Kay and Phil Smith in Barlestone. When I spoke to four of the women in August 2008, Margaret Pinnegar produced the minutes of their first meeting, and was able to tell me that present at the inaugural meeting were Kay Smith, her mother Mary Brearley, Wendy Jeffery, Sue Concannon, Kathy Douglas, Barbara Jeffery, Debbie Mellin, Carol Girvan, Julie Girvan, Rose Elcock and Margaret Pinnegar. Carol was the wife of Bobby Girvan and Julie was married to his brother Sam. There were two Jeffery wives because Barbara was the wife of Cliff, and Wendy was about to marry Cliff's son Nigel.

Kay Smith told me, "Organisations I'd started to work with had been telling me, 'You ought to do this, you ought to do that,' so one day I told Phil that I couldn't just sit at home. I'd got to do something. We all got together at our house, and were given advice from a nurse called Jane Bruton, who came over from Leicester to help us get organised." Jane

Bruton, mentioned earlier, was the secretary of the Leicester Miners Support Group.

All of the women threw themselves into action, although several of the wives were working – and continued to be the only breadwinner for the rest of the year – and of course some of the younger striking miners were not married, and so had no partners on the Women's Group. Kay continued, "I don't know how we came to have the youth centre at Greenhill to store stuff. But people would donate food, and the wives who were at home used to go to the meetings with the blokes. We had somebody donated food, and we put it on a table. We worked out that we'd got something like three tins for each family. But then, as the food collections escalated, it

all ended up in our garage. My youngest lad, I used to put him in a playpen in the middle of the garage and all the stuff was stacked up round the outside. And we each used to go round with a bag.

"They used to come here on a Sunday night. They used to collect in Leicester, then bring the food and put it in the garage. Then as time went on, I started speaking to meetings, Phil used to do the food parcels and take them round in his blue Renault Five, him and Martin Concannon. I remember from time to time we had pop bottles explode, everything ended up dripping and covered in orange pop."

Kay told me that although most people who gave did so because they were supporters of the Dirty Thirty, she could remember a few attempt at sabotage, obviously by someone who disapproved of their activities, someone who was extremely vindictive.

"We had somebody put drawing pins in some porridge. We weren't sure if the packet had been opened or not, and when we checked, we found drawing pins in it. That happened on a few occasions. We had to be aware that not everybody was a supporter. There's people in this village who still don't speak to me to this day. On the other side of the scale, when it was coming up to Christmas, an anonymous £20 came through the door, with a letter saying, 'Here's £20 towards your Christmas.' We'd get old people donate. Those who did the collecting, food and that, they'd come on Sunday night, and sometimes there'd be a little note saying, 'I ain't got much but you can have this.' They were so insistent that they wanted to help.

"You know, the people who you didn't think would support you, did. There were a lot of different groups that supported us. I mean, I was just a housewife supporting the strike. It's not till you look back, you think, 'Bloody Hell, I did that.' But you do it. As time went on, the Women's Group started to raise money for ourselves to take the kids on a daytrip to Drayton Manor."

Margaret Pinnegar told me about Melvyn Pack, a lecturer at Leicester Poly. "When Melvyn got to know we'd got a group, he wanted to do something for the women. So he arranged for us to take the children on a trip. We had to decide where to take them, so we decided to go to London to see the Christmas lights. Also there was something else. We had ten pounds each for the children."

Kay put in, "All the money that we raised was held in a building society – there was a branch of the Hinckley and Rugby in the village – and we had three names on it didn't we? You needed two signatures to draw any money out. We were the nearest, so it was me, Wendy and the third might have been Geraldine Findell. After the strike there was still a bit of money left, so we gave it to Children In Need."

Kay was of a line of mining stock, and it was not surprising that she became one of the more active of the Dirty Thirty women. Her granddad, Herbert Brearley, had been in the 1926 strike, and her father, Johnny Brearley, was in the 1972 and 74 strikes. She recalled with pride, "The old folks weren't getting any coal then, obviously, so they went and chopped down nearly a whole spinney so everybody got some wood to burn. So I knew what was going to happen. It's in my blood I suppose.

"I started on public speaking pretty early on. My first speech was in Leicester and it was only about six lines. My mam and dad were there, and my dad said I spoke too fast. I used to be absolutely petrified. Tommy Murray got up and spoke, next there was me, and then I'm sure it was Peter Heathfield." Peter Heathfield was the NUM national general secretary.

"There weren't that many people there, but I used to get stressed out if I'd got to speak. I used to take two paracetamol half an hour before, and I used to write my speech down word for word – mind you, my spelling weren't brilliant – in letters big enough so that when I stood up I could see it on the table. So that if I got lost I could look down. As time went on, I had to tell them more, to speak for longer, but I never got any less nervous. I don't know what Philip thought of my speaking because I never asked him. I just done it. We didn't have time to ask one another anything. We were passing the kids back and forward between us."

I found I could answer the question that Kay asked. In an interview with Phil, some weeks later, he told me, "Kay was absolutely fantastic, she was so strong. She spoke what she felt. There were no frills, she told it like it was happening. More often than not, she got a standing ovation. When I heard her speak to a meeting, I had a lump in my throat. I used to think, 'That's my missus up there'. It was like I'd won the lottery. She was absolutely fantastic. I was so proud of her."

Kay recalled a visit she made to the Dirty Thirty HQ in Leicester. "The blokes got the strike office in Leicester, above Willie Thorne's snooker hall in Charles Street. Well, I went to see them and I didn't know Charles Street. I went in the building next door and the lift was broke. I carried Lewis in the pushchair up three flights of stairs, and when I got there I realised I was in the wrong building. I had to carry him and the pushchair all the way back down. Then I had to go to the strike office, carrying him all the way up these other stairs again."

Several of the Women's Group had children to care for, as well as becoming activists in the cause. Kathy Douglas had a baby just as the strike was beginning. Carol Girvan had a baby born on Christmas Day, during the strike. Margaret Pinnegar's daughters were older, fifteen and seventeen, but they were still at school and obviously needed at least one parent to be there for them.

At the first meeting of the Women's Group, Kay made a decision that shocked at least one of the Dirty Thirty. She described how, when the men returned to pick up their wives, Benny asked, "How's your meeting gone then, ladies?" I said, "All right." He said, "Have you decided what you're going to do?" I said, "Yes, we're going to picket." He says, "You ain't." He looks at my husband and says, "Tell her, Smithy. She's not going picketing." He says, "I can't do nowt. She'll do what she wants." Malcolm says, "Well, if you get on that picket line, you're on your own. If you get arrested, you get arrested. We can't look after you and look after ourselves as well." So I says, "All right. Fair comment."

Margaret explained that her husband was worried about the women getting knocked about. "He couldn't look after us. I said straightaway that I wasn't going to picket because we couldn't both be arrested. I thought if he's arrested and I'm arrested, then we're in a mess. I must admit I didn't do an awful lot compared with some, because Malcolm was away all the time – I hardly saw him for twelve months – and I had to look after the girls."

However, Kay was determined to go picketing, and she did. She did however take some notice of Malcolm's warning. "I don't think I ever went on a picket line with Phil. If he went picketing, I didn't go. I used to go with Geek and Nigel, because Geek had worked down the pit with my dad until my dad had to finish through ill-health, so Geek and my dad were the best of buddies. The first picket I went on was at Donisthorpe in the South Derbyshire coalfield. I remember Geek said, 'Wait till we get there, I've got something to show you.' He'd got a placard, and as they went through he held it up and he shouted, 'Look at that. What's it say?' And it had got on:

## ARE YOU A MAN OR A MOUSE?

*1985. The Dirty Thirty on a march for the jailed striking miners, led by Bob Girvan's son Stuart.*

51

Kay admits that at first she was a bit naïve. "We'd made a women's banner out of some old sheets and two props. I went across the road with the banner and it was a bit windy. I don't know where the other girls had gone, so I'd got to hold it on my own. There was some bricks that had fell off the wall, so I started to pick them up to stake my banner in this bit of earth and put the bricks round it, so one side would stand up and I could hold the other side. Some of the pickets were shouting, 'Put it down, put it down! They'll arrest you.' This copper just looked at me, and he walked up and said, 'They'll do you for an offensive weapon. Put the brick down.' I was so naïve that I was going, 'What are you on about?' I was doing it in all innocence, but obviously they assumed I was going to chuck it at a lorry. That was my first experience of picketing."

Kath Douglas told me about a frightening experience that did confirm Malcolm's worries about the women. "I didn't do any picketing because we had a new baby, born as the strike was starting. I know Dave didn't want me to go on the picket line – he didn't think it was the place for women – and I didn't really want to go anyway. I'd do anything to support him, but I wasn't going into that. I was a bit like Wendy because I was working. I was a hairdresser and I worked six days a week. We had to get some money from somewhere. But I did go on a march in London. It was just me and Dave that went. I can remember being stranded, because they arrested my old man. I mean, I don't know London that well but I remember going to Bow Street police station, asking if they'd got him. They said, 'No, try such and such.' We went round all these police stations, and it turned out he was in the first one we went to originally, Bow Street. But they were being bloody minded. I was stranded in London. It was horrible. It was like my worst nightmare. It was down Horse Guards Parade. I can remember being pinned to the railings. There was police on horseback, I can remember that. I can't even remember what Dave had done, but whatever he'd done, the police didn't like it. They dragged him off. I was like, 'Oh my God, now what do I do?' We got him out about midnight. They obviously hadn't got anything on him to keep him there, but they wanted to make a point so they kept him in there for so many hours."

Although Margaret Pinnegar never went picketing, her elder daughter did. "I know we went down to South Wales once and Colleen stopped down there when we came home. She slept on the Welsh miners' funds. All the NUM bank accounts had been closed, so they'd got all the money out in cash and she was sleeping on top of the money. And then she went picketing down there. Malcolm and I had a phone call to ask was it all right, she wanted to go picketing. Her dad just said, 'As long as you don't get her arrested, she can go.' So she did do some picketing in South Wales."

Some of the visits to other mining areas were of special interest. Wendy Jeffery and her husband went to an evening do at a place called Doe Lea, on the Derbyshire/Nottinghamshire borders, along with her sister-in-law and her boyfriend. The organiser had asked for some representation from the Dirty Thirty, and when they got there, they said, "See so-and-so and they'll sort you out with accommodation so you don't have to drive back." Wendy explained, "So we all had a drink and got invited back to this chap's house. I think he was single but he'd got his grown up lads living there. Nigel's sister and her boyfriend decided to go and sleep in the car but we went to bed. We got in this bed after staying up for a while and talking. We'd left this guy downstairs, and he'd got a fairly big living room. When we woke up in the morning, this guy hadn't slept. He'd stripped all his walls and repapered his living room all through the night. The room looked entirely different. We just killed ourselves laughing. We just couldn't believe it. We did meet some characters." The Dirty Thirty regarded the miners of Doe Lea with considerable respect because, although the pit there was in private ownership, the miners had joined the strike.

One of the main reasons for visiting other areas was to spread the news about the existence of the Dirty Thirty. Kay and Margaret went to a national women's conference in Barnsley. Kay recalled, "Malcolm took us up and fetched us back. Me and Margaret sat on a wall talking, and we heard one of the women say that there weren't no miners on strike in Leicestershire. So I said, 'Excuse me but there is.' Later we were talking to Nottinghamshire miners' wives and even they didn't know. But by the time we'd done, all the areas knew about the Dirty Thirty."

Another reason for visiting other mining areas was to recharge the batteries, to find out what life was like in a coalfield where the miners were solidly behind the strike. Kay explained, "We were isolated here, so we looked forward to going to these places like South Wales where we were with the majority.

We weren't the minority, like in Leicestershire. At their women's meetings, we could sit and talk about things. We could let our guard down. It gave us a boost."

Margaret commented on how important it was that the children didn't miss out when it came to Christmas, and Wendy added that she ended up with a garage full of presents, some new, some second hand. Leicester City Council agreed to provide a present for each child. The women couldn't remember the source, but they had money from somewhere. Margaret recalled that it was £10 per child, plus a tin of biscuits, a bottle of sherry and some Christmas wrapping paper for each family. Kay reminisced, "I know two kids that weren't expecting anything. One of them was my eldest son Brendan and one was Dean, Barbara's youngest son. All Brendan had asked for was a little portable black and white telly. And when he got up on Christmas morning, he came downstairs shaking from head to foot because he's got that much stuff. It was just unbelievable. He got his telly and quite a lot of other things, not all brand new, some were second hand. We weren't greedy, we got in touch with head office, the women's group, to find out what areas hadn't got anything. We got a van and we took them, and distributed them ourselves. Some went to Chesterfield in North Derbyshire. We also sent food to South Wales, because we'd got enough."

Kay's increasing confidence and her ability as a speaker meant that she was soon in demand. "All these different women's organisations wanted someone from our group to speak to them. They wanted to know how we were struggling in the strike. It continued even after the strike had ended. There are some people out there who have contacted me since the strike – I don't even know how they've got my name and number, it's obviously word of mouth – and they've wanted to know about the women in the miners' strike. Some of them are even doing it as a course in their A levels, I think."

Kay did feel uncomfortable on a couple of occasions. "When we went to the national women's meetings in Sheffield there was this delegate from South Derbyshire – Sue. Ann Scargill used to sit where her husband usually sat and Betty Heathfield would sit where Peter normally sat. We were told to sit where the men NUM delegates from our area usually sat. But Sue from South Derbyshire and me, we refused to sit where Jack Jones and Ken Toon had been, because they were scab leaders."

The other occasion was when, after the strike, Wendy, Kathy and Kay went to a meeting held on a university campus. They were annoyed to find that the national women's group wanted to invite wives of the miners who had worked during the strike to join them. "It was when the strike was over, and they wanted all the people – the wives of the men who hadn't been on strike – they wanted to accept them back into the fold. I said, 'I can't do it. We've gone without for a year, and you're telling me we've now got to accept them. Well, I can't.' It was to bring the NUM back as a whole, to encourage them to come back. I couldn't vote for that so I abstained from voting. And when they got up and sang that bloody song, "We are women, we are strong" I just couldn't join in. One of our supporters, Viv from Chesterfield, was in the audience and she said, 'I could see from the look on your face that you weren't happy.' I didn't mind the song itself, but it was at the end of this meeting, where we expected to unite as one. But we'd gone without, they hadn't gone without anything. The scabs' wives weren't there, but the women's organisation wanted to encourage them to join, to keep the groups going. I was dead against it. They wanted to say, 'Well now it's over, we can set up united women's groups for this or that.' They didn't want the groups to disband. Ours did, because everybody went back to work, went about their own business once the strike was finished."

Kay's resolute attitude to scabs was echoed by Margaret, who recalled, "We had gone to Nottingham for a meeting and went for a drink at a house belonging to a striking miner. While we were there, a man came in with a big bag of coal, and a bag of fruit and vegetables. I said, "That's kind of him," and was then told the man was their next door neighbour and he was a working miner! He was keeping them going with coal and veg. I was speechless. I couldn't have taken it. I would rather have been cold."

Linda Richmond, who became an active member of the Wives' Support Group, did have some doubts along the way. In an article she wrote for a broadsheet published by Ashby Labour Party, she wrote,

*"As a wife of a miner on strike in a minority area, this year has been the hardest of my life. It started on Thursday 15th March when my husband Mick, probably better known as Richo, came home and informed me that he was on strike and would not cross picket lines. I didn't really understand and didn't really agree with him at the time. Mick tried to explain what was what, but I was scared and*

*didn't take much notice. It soon became obvious that Mick was serious, because within three weeks the phone was ringing virtually non-stop. The pressure on me just got too much, and I had to go away to my mother's to escape from the life our daughter Emma and I were leading. I needed to think. After ten days, I decided I would return and try to understand this terrible strike. It was only when Mick was called to a meeting in South Wales that it hit home to me. He took me along because I was low. After meeting the brave people of the Valleys, my mind was absolutely made up. I realised what the fight was all about: jobs, communities, the very way of life. Mick and I still have arguments, but I try to understand. He is under pressure as it is, organising and attending meetings. Some weeks I'm lucky to see him for a day or two. But he will not give in and neither will I. The weeks turn into months, but we remain solid and firm and committed to the cause. I hope it all ends soon. I do not know what lies ahead but I do know I married a man not a scab. Our daughter can one day be proud of her daddy in the knowledge that he and the rest of the Dirty Thirty fought for their jobs, fought for the NUM, and fought for the whole working class. As Mick would say, Victory to the Miners!"*

Linda supported Richo loyally throughout the strike, though they did split up some years later.

*A Dirty Thirty wives reunion in 2004.*

# Trouble and Strife

Not all the memories of the year-long strike were tales of picket line drama and morale-building visits to areas where the Dirty Thirty were regarded with respect and affection. There was hardship too, especially in the early weeks of the strike. Mel Elcock was one who mentioned how difficult it was before the fundraising kicked in. "After 25 years, it's easy to forget the hardship of it. True hardship. I was a regular churchgoer at that time, and my vicar from Thorpe Acre church came to visit me. He could see that we weren't having the easiest of times, and he wanted to give me something to help me out. Well, I'd got three children and they all needed shoes, and the vicar bought three pairs of shoes for my children. Also, every week I received an envelope through the post with two pound notes in it, anonymous, but with a local postmark. I don't know who it was from. The level of support we received was fantastic from an area that was almost solidly working. A year can go in a flash, but that year didn't. It was a long long year. You get to thinking at times, how long are we going to go on?

"I was getting letters from the bank, saying 'Yet again we draw your attention to the deficit in your account.' And yet the same day, I received a letter saying, 'As a valued customer, you can now have a loan of up to £30,000.' I wrote back and said, 'Take out what I owe you and send me the rest!' Needless to say, I didn't get any response. Obviously we'd got a mortgage on the house, but luckily my wife worked fulltime, she worked in hosiery. That just – only just – kept our heads above water. But I was still in the red at the bank. I'd been down to the bank and explained to the manager. I didn't wait for him to come and see me. However, when we went back to work, everything we drew was tax free. All of a sudden we became the envy of everybody. We paid no tax. When we went back to work, in March 85, everything we drew up to the next tax year was tax free, because we'd earned nothing during the year of the strike. We were rich for a while then. It was a case of paying the debts off and putting the house in order again."

Dave Douglas was another of the Dirty Thirty who had trouble with his bank, but his problems came after the strike! "During the strike, I was with the TSB then for my mortgage, and the bank sympathised. They said, 'We understand that you're on strike, don't worry about it, when you go back to

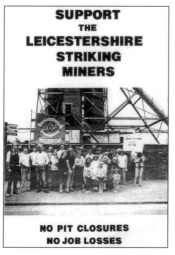

work we'll sort it out.' During the strike the bank was all right, but when the strike was over, within my first week's wage packet time, I was getting demand letters from the bank – the TSB – demanding I pay the arrears in full. It was over a period of time, but it was ridiculous, less than a year. I was living in Stoneygate at the time. I had no choice but to sell my house, the first home I'd bought. It was the only way I could pay the bank what I owed them. Originally it was an £18,000 mortgage, but I hadn't paid mortgage for twelve months being on strike, so it had accumulated a load of interest on top of that. I ended up owing them a lot more than what I borrowed, and I had to sell the house. I did manage to raise a mortgage to buy another house, but I had to sell that one to raise the money. I never used the TSB ever again. You see, if it had been the Yorkshire Bank, in a striking area, they wouldn't have been able to do that. Maybe I should have been with the Yorkshire Bank or the old Bank of Wales."

Dave's wife, Kath, had a job as a hairdresser, which brought in some income, and Wendy Jeffery worked in an insurance office. Other strikers had different ways of making ends meet. John Gamble was a part-time bookmaker, and would occasionally leave a rally early to go off to an evening race meeting. John's expertise and knowledge of horseracing did come in useful after the strike. He was able to give members of the Dirty Thirty some valuable tips, including the winner of the Grand National, Last Suspect, which came in at 66/1.

Wag Burton had a rather useful dog. "During the strike I had a lurcher and I used to go rabbiting with Jim Chambers. Jim was a good lad to me. He'd been a miner, but by the time of the strike he was a gamekeeper at Swithland Reservoir. We used to go over to Grantham, because a farmer there was overrun with rabbits. It was unbelievable. I'd never seen so many. We'd come back with sixty rabbits, clean them up and take them up to Coalville, where the old market used to be, at the Red House. People used to be waiting for Jim pulling up on Saturday morning with his rabbits. He used to sell them up there, then come down Whitwick. We'd only get a quid for each rabbit. I had one or two for food, and I'd sell a few up the pub. I used to give some to the old folks, and I hadn't used to charge them.

"I'd got three kids when the strike started, Clare, Damion and Lynsey, so the rabbits I caught came in useful. My parents would help me out here and there, and Sue's parents did too. They were behind me, although Sue's aunty, who was very good looking after Clare, when Sue told her we'd got no sugar for the kids' cornflakes, she just said, 'Tell Wag to get back to work then.' All my brothers used to help us out. They'd been miners but they weren't at the pit at the time. They'd moved out into other jobs, but I know that they'd have come out if they were still mining. They wouldn't have scabbed. My dad would have told them to. We didn't get a lot of money from the fundraising. It were very hard. We were scraping here and there, trying to make ends meet. Some days I used to get up and I was full of it, and then a couple of days later I was right down, depressed, not knowing if I were doing the right thing. I go to bed and think about it, and I'd decide that I knew it was right."

Although Sue and Wag's children didn't actually like eating rabbit, they could be tricked into it. Sue told me that after Christmas 1985, they were eating up the remains of the turkey, and she decided to make a turkey and rabbit curry. The kids cleared their plates, asked for seconds, before she told them that they had eaten rabbit. Sue also told me how much she appreciated the food parcels, brought round by Phil Smith each week.

It was different for the young single lads. Darren Moore told me that because he lived at home with his parents, he had "a steak pie strike." Like Darren, Nigel Jeffery was single. "Looking back, I suppose it was easy for me, because I was 23 and living with my dad and my stepfamily." Others who were single – Mick Poli, Johnny Gamble – were in a better position to manage than those who were married with a family. Bob Girvan had a young son – he was to have a second one, a "strike baby", on Christmas Day 1984. Wag Burton had three children, as did Mel Elcock. Phil and Kay Smith had two. Gordon Smith tells me that he was a single parent bringing up five teenagers on his own, and his decision to strike was only taken after a family discussion with his children. Kath Douglas had her first child at the beginning of April, just as the strike was beginning. Dave went into hospital to see her and the baby – and to tell her he was on strike.

As the months went on, the Dirty Thirty got so good at both fundraising and collecting food donations, the Leicestershire miners were able to send food to more hardpressed mining areas. Locally the food was to be shared between thirty families; in other areas there were thousands of families to be catered for. Mel Elcock recalled, "The food collections were that good – we'd got that much food – that we supplied other areas and other pits. And out of the money we collected – we were collecting for the strike, not just for us – we used some of it to hire Luton vans, fill them full of food and take it to another area. We went to South Wales, we went to

Durham, and we took food to north Derbyshire and Yorkshire. It was quite a few tons of food."

Bob Girvan recalled having a problem with the Benefits office in Coalville when he went to ask whether he was entitled to any money for his young son. He was told that although he was not unemployed, he should fill in forms for unemployment benefit. "They actually wanted me to go on the dole," he said. He was also told that refusing to cross a picket line was a matter of personal choice. Bob tried to explain that conscience and choice were not the same thing, and that as a trade unionist he could not cross a picket line. He then received a bizarre questionnaire from the manager of the local Coalville Benefits Office asking some very strange questions, including "Who advised you not to cross the picket line on 9/4/84?" Another question was, "Has the picket line been continually in force on each day since 9/4/84, and if not, did you resume work on the days when it was not in force? If you did not, please give your reasons." This questionnaire was obviously from someone who did not understand the first thing about the motives and principles of trade unionism, and Bob's experience was actually featured in two national newspapers.

Some of the Dirty Thirty also faced intimidation and harassment from the working miners. Sam Girvan told me, "I was only about 5′4″ but nobody ever said anything to me in the street. However, I got a couple of threatening calls when I wasn't in. I'd come home from Northampton and Julie would be upset because we'd had a few phone calls saying that things would happen to me when I went back to work. Just silly people. We'd upset a few people."

64

Phil Smith added, "Some people would speak to us, some would not, but I didn't let them bother me."

Nigel Jeffrey told me, "You'd get women taking their kids to school and we'd get abused. Round here, we were actually called the scabs! It was so ironic that they were classing us as scabs. On a few occasions, we had things thrown at the windows, eggs and so on. We had only just moved into Barlestone, but they knew we were Dirty Thirty because we used to go out drinking with the visiting pickets, and their minibus was parked outside. I suppose looking back we could have kept a low profile but we were proud of what we were doing. Why should we feel embarrassed to go out? It was something we believed in and we did it for twelve months."

Dave Douglas and Mel Elcock, living in Leicester and Loughborough respectively didn't face any of the intimidation. Mel explained, "Personally, I didn't get any harassment from working miners because Loughborough wasn't a mining town. We did see violence on the picket line – mostly perpetrated by the police, which people at that time would not believe, but the truth has come out now. Malcolm was the only one, as far as I know, that was actually attacked and that was in his own home."

Mel was referring to an event of 17th November 1984, when a working miner came to Malcolm Pinnegar's house in Stoney Stanton, pushed his way in and tried to beat him up. It was at 2am, long after pub closing time, which may have been significant. Earlier in the evening the man had been verbally abusing Malcolm's daughter in the local club, so it may not have been entirely unexpected when he came round "to sort Malcolm out." The man did not succeed, though he did punch and headbutt him. Malcolm managed to grab the intruder, pushed him to the ground and sat on him while Margaret rang for the police. Normally in the case of a scuffle between a working miner and a striking miner, the authorities sided with the scab, whoever had started the trouble. There are innumerable cases in Nottinghamshire where a fight between a scab and a striker in the local Welfare had led to the sacking of the striker, even when everyone could see he had not started the fight. However, in Malcolm's case what may have swayed the police was the fact that the assailant had come to Malcolm's house with a gang of cronies. They had waited outside, no doubt hoping that Malcolm and their mate would come outside to fight, and they would be able to join in. When the police car arrived, the police went into the house, and the men waiting outside decided to take off the handbrake of the police car, and let the vehicle roll down the hill. Not a sensible move. The assailant was charged with Actual Bodily Harm. Malcolm recalled that all the local area officials were in court to support his attacker. Some of the Dirty Thirty were also there, and Malcolm is very proud of the way his wife gave evidence. At one stage Malcolm was concerned that he – the victim of the assault – could himself be bound over, which would have curtailed his Dirty Thirty activities. Fortunately this didn't happen and the accused man was found guilty and fined. Sad to report, his fine was paid for by other working miners taking a collection at the pit. They obviously approved of the violent action the man had taken.

Although the Dirty Thirty were not appreciated by the majority of Leicestershire miners, in many

66

other coalfields they were regarded as heroes. One Yorkshire miner, Dave Barker of Armthorpe pit, penned these words of tribute:

## A Tribute to the Dirty Thirty

Of all the struggles that I've known
In all the history of the working class,
There are thirty men from Leicestershire
Whose courage will never be surpassed.

They have faced up to the riot squads,
The scabs and the courts,
But no matter what the bribe will be
The Dirty Thirty can't be bought.

Day in, day out, they carry on
And heed their union call.
Their message to all miners
Is to fight for jobs for all.

They'll never bow to Thatcher,
McGregor and the rest,
For they know with Scargill's leadership
They are the very best.

Living up here in Yorkshire
Scabs are not often found,
But in Leicestershire where the Thirty live
It's the opposite way round.

For it's easy to fight in Yorkshire
When you've a thousand mates or more,
But if you're one of the Thirty
You've a scab at every door.

So when this long battle is over,
We must never desert men so brave,
For shoulder to shoulder they've stood by us
In the fight for our pits to save.

So come on you miners from Leicestershire
Get off your knees and fight,
For time will prove in years to come
It's the Thirty who got it right.

# Spreading the Word

One of the main tasks of the Dirty Thirty was to spread the word throughout the land – telling people what the strike was all about, and pointing out that there were miners in Leicestershire who were on strike. Malcolm and Richo spent a lot of their time travelling to other mining areas to tell them about the Dirty Thirty. One day they'd be speaking at a Sikh temple in Leicester, where they collected hundreds of pounds in donations, and another addressing a Labour Party meeting in Birstall, described by Malcolm as "a fantastic branch." One of the first places they visited was Pontypridd in South Wales, where they visited every mining valley. Richo laughed and told me that at one meeting Malcolm made his opening remarks in Welsh, written down and learnt word for word. The Welsh miners really applauded him.

Richo recalled, "I went up to Bold in Lancashire, and spoke to them. Dave Douglas came with me. They didn't believe there was anybody on strike in Leicestershire. Later we went up to Scotland. Linda had been up to see her father and she'd put some money in a collection tin for the striking miners. When she said her husband was a striking miner in Leicestershire, they just laughed. So I wrote to the *Scots Miner* newspaper, and that's how we got known in Scotland." Malcolm, Richo and Darren Moore went to Scotland to meet the miners there. Malcolm reminisced, "The visit to Scotland was an

LEICESTERSHIRE STRIKING MINERS

NO SURRENDER

Hardship, but 'no surrender'

Unseen cost of policing picket line

SIMILAR?

but who's suffering the most?

SUPPORT THE MINERS

'THE DIRTY THIRTY'

NO SURRENDER

The badge of courage!

'THE DIRTY THIRTY'

NO SURRENDER

'A Strike-breaker is a traitor'

Jack London's definition of a Scab.

LEICESTERSHIRE STRIKING MINERS

**THE MINERS' FIGHT FOR JOBS
IS OUR FIGHT TOO**

*DON'T LET THEM STAND ALONE!*

Law and Order in the Coalfields

FLAMBO

*SUPPORT THE 'DIRTY THIRTY'*

*LEICS STRIKING*

**'THE DIRTY THIRTY'
LEICESTERSHIRE STRIKING MINERS**

**WITH YOUR HELP THEY SHALL NOT STARVE!**

**TRADE UNIONISTS**

AFTER THE T.U.C. ~
WHERE DO WE GO FROM HERE?

# Public Meeting

+ Videos

Speakers :-
  Bob McSporran  (N.U.M. Powergroup President)
  Eddie Martin  (N.G.A. National Officer)
  John Shipp  (C.P.S.A. National Executive)
  Phil Barnard  (EETPU . T.U.C. Delegate)

Plus Videos on Miners & N.G.A. disputes.

**MONDAY SEPT. 10th
Labour Hall
New Bradwell    8PM.**

**ALL WELCOME**

Organised by Milton Keynes Miners Support Group.

education in itself. The sectarianism was very evident. Although miners worked at the same pit, Polmaise, there was a Catholic Miners Welfare and a separate Protestant Miners Welfare. They even lived in separate villages. The Protestant miners lived in Fallin and the Catholics lived in Cowie, but they were both superb in their support for the strike. There weren't no messing about with these strike leaders, be they Protestants or Catholics. We joined a Scottish miners' rally, but there were peculiar things going on, on sectarian lines. This sectarianism was completely alien to us."

Recalling the same visit, Darren Moore said, "I remember, me, Benny and Richo went up to Ayrshire and Fife in Scotland, in the area of Polmaise pit. I was very impressed with the way they were organised. They didn't mess about, they just said, 'Who's picketing today?' and a load of hands went up, including this great big bloke who said he was. They said, 'Well I don't think you should go picketing today because you're in court at ten.' He still wanted to go and picket though. The people were still really enthusiastic, and this was quite a way through the strike. I mean, there was one guy in the Miners Welfare who they wouldn't talk to. I said, 'Why wouldn't anyone talk to him?' and they said, 'Well, he's signed on the dole.' I said, 'He's not gone back to work then?' They said, 'No, but he's gone and signed on the dole.' That was enough for them."

From Scotland, the Dirty Thirty leaders went down to the Durham coalfields, and then into Yorkshire. In the North-East, there was a lot of hardship in evidence. Malcolm told me that they went to the home of one miner where they had sold all the furniture to make ends meet. "We visited one bloke's house at Westoe, where they hadn't got no tables. Some of the families didn't have any food to give us a meal. To us it was mind-blowing. It was like going back to the Victorian age. They had nothing."

Malcolm and Richo were renowned for having very different speaking styles. Malcolm said, "My talks were always very political. The strike was always a political thing to me. My interest was in winning the strike. I was very frustrated because of these blokes who didn't seem to understand. Even a lot of miners who were on strike thought that it was just about securing the future of the pits. But to me and to Darren it was a political thing. Darren gave up his future really because he'd been training for pit management, but he was following his conscience." While Malcolm always gave the hardline political talks, Richo would talk about the hardship that the miners were going through. "Benny was more political than me. Basically I was telling them about the families and how we were struggling, and saying that we were absolutely surrounded in Coalville by working miners. I was desperately worried about how we were all going to survive." Malcolm used to laugh and call Richo's style hearts-and-flowers, but in truth the combination of the two types of speech blended into a powerful argument, some listeners reacting to one, and others to the other. Malcolm admits that his scorn was entirely misplaced. "I didn't appreciate until after the strike, exactly what difference Richo made with his hearts-and-flowers. I gave him that name because at the time I didn't like the way he did speeches, but I was proved to be completely and absolutely wrong."

Both Richo and Malcolm were unceasing in the hours they put in. Malcolm told me, "I never stopped, I was doing three jobs a day. I went to hundreds of different meetings." A look at the diary that Richo kept during the strike convinced me that he was putting in many more hours per day than when he was down the pit, frequently getting home after midnight, and getting up at 5.30 the next morning to go picketing.

One of the places where members of the Dirty Thirty used to visit was Northampton, raising money and spreading the word. Dave Douglas told me, "I was in Northampton now and again, collecting, just for a break, to get out of the Leicester office, but the Girvans were there almost every week. I think that was their second home, by the end of it."

Bob Girvan confirmed this. "Me, my brother Sam, John Gamble, Mick Poli, young Billy Scott, Waggy Burton and especially Geordie Bob, we were in Northampton all the time. As it went on a bit, instead of staying there the full week, I'd only stay a couple of days because Carol was pregnant. The first day we went up to Northampton, it was a good bit into the strike, and it was a really hot sunny day. I think we'd been up there a day or two, and we met a lad called Bill Fleming from the Communist Party. Bill was very politically acute – I'd be talking to someone, trying to get contacts, and he'd say, "He's S.O." I thought he meant petrol, Esso, but he meant Socialist Organiser. Bill took us to a hospital and to a fire station, and their unions gave us some donations."

Bob's brother, Sam, added, "They were great people, weren't they. There were the Labour people, then the Trotskyists and the Communists who didn't get on with each other, but they were all supporting us. Wherever we went, we were made more than welcome. It didn't bother us what party people were in. I wasn't a member of any party, but I do vote Labour because it's a class vote. We'd go and talk to the men in a factory canteen, then stand at the gates giving out leaflets and speaking to them, with a bucket on the floor for them to chuck money in."

One event organised in Northampton was a public meeting at the Guild Hall. One of the speakers was Tony Benn, who recorded in his diary: "16th October 1984: Caught the train to Northampton. I was taken to the Guild Hall where there was a committee of people who were planning the meeting and a press conference, all very well organised. There are only thirty out of the 2500 Leicestershire Miners on strike, and they are known as the 'dirty thirty,' and yet they organised the meeting, which I was told was the biggest political meeting ever held in Northampton. There were about 700 or 800 people there. The chair was the Regional Secretary of UCATT, the builders' union, and then there was Chris Jones from the Arkwright Colliery in North Derbyshire and one of the Leicestershire miners who delivered a violent attack on the scabs. The class nature of the speeches was much sharper than I have ever heard before, and the audience was full of response. It was really interesting to see the advancement of political education and the response of the audience. Kay Smith from the Dirty Thirty

Wives' Group was extremely powerful." The Leicester-shire miner referred to in Tony's diary was Malcolm Pinnegar.

Sam Girvan recalled, "We met some lovely people who put us up, and one of the first nights we were there we were staying with a couple called Ruth and Dave Walters. And what was good about it, Ruth and Dave would open their house to us. It was a free house. I'd say so-and-so was coming next week, and they'd make room. You could go in and make your-self something to eat. They were brilliant, fantastic. We can't thank those people enough. We were all in Ruth and Dave's one time, and this woman from the next street came in. Ruth says, 'Oh, these are my Leicestershire miners,' and her friend looks at us and says, 'Oh, well, where's my miners?' The two young lads, Billy Scott and Mick Poli, they really did well, and so did young Chunky, Alan Findell, Geek's stepson. They had a lot to do at Northampton. The way they collected was unbelievable."

Bob then laughed and told me that in North-ampton, people were not used to miners and some had a stereotypical image of what a miner would be like. "We were sort of aliens. A lot of these people when they first saw us – and I don't mean it to be rude – they expected us to have flat caps and a whippet. One night, they organised a quiz night to raise funds for us. It was at the NALGO union club in Northampton – University Challenge. We had a team, the university lecturers had a team, and there was a team of teachers. And we beat them hands down. They just couldn't believe it."

Bob told me that a teacher from Countesthorpe College in Leicestershire, introduced them to her mother, June Chenewell, who lived in Marlborough in Wiltshire. "June actually wanted to start a support group down there, so myself, young Mick Poli and a lad called Barry Draycott who was a union official, we went down to Wiltshire. June put us up and she told us she was a Quaker. The irrepressible Mick said to her, 'You don't look like they do on the Porridge Oats packet.' June's American husband had been a big union man and he'd been jailed under McCarthyism. I never met him, and I think perhaps he was deceased. What we did, we went into schools and gave talks. I'd do the family man thing, Barry did the union statistics because he was very precise on policy and procedure, and Mick would tell the picket line stories. It was like a travelling show in a way. The kids loved young Mick because he had no hair – it was through alopecia, but the kids thought he was a skinhead. In one school they did like a project on us. They let us speak, and then after that it caught their imagination. What was really touching about the visit to Wiltshire, they kept sending us donations and correspondence from the school. Just before Christmas 1984, I got a card from a lad called Neil. He'd saved up all his pocket money and sent it, saying that he wanted me to get a Christmas present with it. It about broke my heart. You can't even begin to repay that kindness. But you can't forget it."

Nigel Jeffery was less keen on Northampton than some of the others, telling me, "I wasn't that keen going down there. One time I went wasn't that enjoyable. I remember collecting there, and we'd be wearing stickers with *Coal, Not Dole* and *Support the Miners*. There was actually an old guy there with banners and he was collecting on behalf of the working miners! He used to stand near deliberately, trying to disrupt us. He was a member of the Conservative Party, and he was doing everything in his power to put people off. He'd got a banner saying, *Support Margaret Thatcher, Support the Working Miners,* and *The Striking Miners are Evil.* So I never enjoyed it.

"The one chap that made me enjoy it was a lad called Higgins, Brian Higgins. He was a massive Scots lad that had been blacklisted throughout the building sites for trying to organise unions. It was a regular thing down in Northampton because of the workers at LaBour Pumps. They'd been on strike more or less the same length of time as us. So as well as collecting on behalf of the miners, some of the proceeds would go towards these LaBour Pump workers. The majority of them were out, and there were only one or two scabs still going in. On this particular occasion, I'd gone down, taking a car load of pickets from Durham with me. They did say that there were going to be a lot of people on the picket line. We were there early – six o'clock in the morning – and there was between fifty and a hundred people there picketing. It was a good crowd.

"Of course this Brian Higgins stands out because he was 6´6´´ plus. I'm 6´2´´ and he towered over me. He was a big lad, as broad as he was tall, and he had a great big moustache like Lech Walesa. He was loud, very loud. I remember standing on this picket line, and one car had gone in. There was a lot of pushing and shoving going on, and there were two or three vans of Northamptonshire police. Then we saw up the road in the distance these other police marching, coming over the hill. There were hundreds of them. Talk about military. This is what we've always said, it was the army dressed up as police. They came marching down the road, military style, and as soon as they got to us, they all linked arms and started pushing us back. They were trying to separate people into small groups.

"Then there must have been half a dozen police went for this Brian Higgins, and snatched him. They just grabbed him for no particular reason other than he was shouting his protest. He hadn't done anything wrong, as far as we could see. He was shoving them off left right and centre. They were trying to drag him down the road, and I went to intervene, trying to say that he'd done nothing. That's when I then got three or four police turn on me. They had my arms up my back, and they pulled me backwards up against this fence. As they were holding my arms, two to each arm, I got a bit of a kicking and a bit of punching in the stomach. I was then hauled into a van, and taken to Wellingborough. One of the conditions of my bail was not to set foot in Wellingborough. I have been back since with my present job, lorry driving, and I remember that I used to be banned from there. When we went to court, the police let themselves down. I knew I'd done nothing wrong, but if they'd got their stories straight, I probably would have been done for whatever they were alleging. I can remember them coming into the box, one at a time, giving contradictory evidence. It was farcical, to hear them all saying different things. They contradicted one another on when the police wrote up their notes, and whether the inspector had come in the van with them. One of the magistrates even tried to make out that I had superhuman strength. The police were trying to say in their notebooks that it took six policemen to restrain me because I was running up the road dragging them with me. It was completely false. So on their evidence, they just shot themselves in the foot, so I was discharged."

Darren Moore went to Milton Keynes to raise funds and spread the word, "I was sent to fundraise in Milton Keynes with the South Derbyshire and Staffordshire miners for about 8-12 weeks, coming back at weekends. I used to go down there on a Monday and I often used to stay for the week with this couple – Rose and Pete Bailey. They used to take us out collecting on the estates at night. Then if there were meetings, I'd go and speak. I ran a marathon to raise money and I've still got the medal I had from the Mayor for completing the course. The money we raised was shared out between the different groups of miners. We were starting to become accomplished at fundraising so after a while we left collecting in Milton Keynes to the other groups. I also did stints in Northampton and

*Christmas cards produced and sold to raise funds for the Dirty Thirty, December 1984.*

went to London collecting door to door in Hackney. Some of the people we collected off in the tower blocks were so poor I wanted to give them money!

"I spent a lot of time in Milton Keynes and most of it was great. Different people fed us every night and because they were supporters we often used to get a good meal. I can remember somebody who ran the Woodcraft Folk gave us a meal and they cooked us steak! I couldn't believe it. We were well looked after and it boosted morale to know we were not alone. Not everybody supported the miners. I had to speak at Aylesbury NALGO because the branch had put a motion forward to have a levy taken out of everybody's wages to go to the striking miners. Well, there's no mines round there and it's a fairly right wing area. Aylesbury NALGO had a massive membership and this meeting was packed out. It was a big hall, and there must have been six hundred there, which is pretty unusual for a union meeting, but the majority had come to make sure they didn't have the levy for the miners. I didn't go down particularly well there because I still gave then the political message. I could feel the meeting was not going our way, and some were quite hostile. Someone even got up and said, 'We ought to sell the Welsh miners' houses off for holiday homes,' being really flippant. The motion didn't get passed but it was an experience."

# Tales from the Picket Line

One of the main tasks undertaken by the Dirty Thirty was of course picketing. It was important that the four Leicestershire working pits – Bagworth, South Leicester, Whitwick, Ellistown, plus the former pit at Nailstone, where coal from the four pits was screened and despatched – should be picketed every day. This was sometimes a token picket, but at times the Dirty Thirty numbers were boosted by support groups and by pickets from other areas including South Wales, Kent and County Durham.

Not surprisingly, many of the reminiscences of the Dirty Thirty are related to incidents that happened on the picket line. One that made me laugh was told to me by Cliff Jeffery, a.k.a. Geek. "Although on the whole, picketing was disappointing and grim, sometimes it did have a lighter side. I can recall one such incident. I joined the picket line at Nailstone one morning. Coal was being screened from Bagworth Colliery and being transported away in lorries. Quite a large crowd of striking miners from Notts had gathered. Whenever there's a crowd there's always a joker among it, and today was no exception. Jumping on and off lorries, he was doing his utmost to persuade the drivers to turn round. After several unsuccessful attempts he turned to the crowd and announced loudly, 'I've got an idea. I'm not having much luck this way so from now on I'm going to hypnotise the fuckers.' When the next lorry pulled up he jumped on the running board, looked directly at the driver, and began his spiel. 'Look into my eyes, look into my eyes. You are going to turn round.' The driver promptly told him to 'Fuck off, you silly bugger.' After several more amusing encounters the joker turned to the crowd and announced, 'I give up. The fuckers are brain dead.' "

Bob and Sam Girvan recalled that Cliff had "one of those caravanettes, like a Scoobydoo wagon." Cliff's wagon became the mobile canteen. Cliff told me, "At the time I came out on strike I owned a Volkswagen caravanette, which came in handy for providing hot bacon and sausage butties to the lads on the picket line. My wife would visit the Co-op and stock up with baps, etc, and the next morning at Nailstone Colliery the frying pan and grill would be working overtime to meet the demand. We had previously worked out the price of each bap so as not to make any profit. My conscience would never allow me to rip off my colleagues, Dirty Thirty or otherwise. The van also became useful for ferrying a few of the lads to different picketing sites. One day during the summer, it was decided a few of the Dirty Thirty would picket at Moira. The following morning I picked up all the lads and off we set. We were aware that there was a strong possibility of being stopped by the police, so we decided to take the backroads. We got that wrong. Four miles from the pit a police car was blocking the road. We were informed that there was already a big picket at the pit, and if I attempted to drive on I would be arrested. My mates decided to walk the rest of the way. When they got to the pit there was no one there. I joined them later when the police moved on. The lying bastards."

Cliff's son Nigel had a tale to tell about his arrest on a picket line at Rawdon colliery, in Moira. Although Moira is in Leicestershire, Rawdon pit is classed as a South Derbyshire colliery. Nigel told me, "I don't know why we picked out Rawdon. When we'd had our weekly meetings, we picked out which were the places we were going to target. At times there'd be police roadblocks, and obviously they recognised our cars and turned us back. Anyway we were picketing Rawdon on this particular day, and I'd gone along with my father and my stepmother. There were other women there on the picket line. When we actually got to Rawdon, they made us stand across the road from the entrance. I think there were only one or two miners allowed to go across and speak to the cars going in. The police were actually from the Met and they were very – how can you say – very *orchestrated*. At earlier pickets, even up at Nailstone, some of the local bobbies had quite a bit of sympathy for us. Many a time we had the police turn round and say, 'Well my dad, my granddad, used to work in the pit, and he was on strike.'

"But that day, there was just a bad feeling about it at Rawdon. I just sensed that something was going to kick off. It was as though they were there for a reason. At the time we were more or less finishing. We had been shouting some things, to give our support, trying to get these people to turn round. But it was a friendly family atmosphere with the women, including my stepmother, and my dad being there. My dad and I had a lot of respect for each other.

"Then towards the end, a handful of police literally marched across the road, military-style, and two or three of them went one way and the others came towards me. At the time I was just sitting down, talking to a miner from Nottinghamshire. Two came either side of me, grabbed my arms, and pushed them up my back. Everybody said, 'What's happening. What are you doing? What has he done?' Nobody would actually say what we'd done. I got chucked into the back of this van, chucked on the floor, and as they all sat around I'm lying on the floor, and I'm getting kicked and stamped on. It was a very scary experience. I'd never gone through that before, never been in trouble with the police. I was always brought up to respect the police. When I was a kid, I was told if you ever get lost, the first one you go and see is a policeman. I don't know why I was picked out. Whether I was shouting the most, I've no idea. But at the worst, the only thing I was shouting was Scab. Billy Scott was arrested at the same time. We were brought down to Coalville police station, where the local bobbies were actually embarrassed and apologetic. These Met blokes had dumped us, dragged us out the vans, punching and pinching us, and escorted us into the cells. When they'd gone, the local police said, 'We're sorry. It's nothing to do with us. These are from the Met.' Even they were calling them, saying they were animals. The Met police used to taunt us, telling us how much they were earning on overtime. That was the first time I was arrested."

Nigel was falsely accused of shouting obscene abuse – 'you fucking scab-carrying bitch' – at a woman taking her husband into work, which he totally denied. "I mean I wouldn't swear in front of my dad, other than down the pit, let alone in front of the women. I was found not guilty, through the court system, in the longest ever case held in Coalville court."

Bob Girvan told me of one amusing incident at Rawdon colliery. "We used to have a chap come by speeding on a Honda 50, speeding past every single day and putting the V signs up. We shouted, 'Scab!' at him, and he loved it. One day he took a corner too fast and he ploughed three coppers up. I thought that was very funny."

The shouting of the word *Scab* was ruled by the courts as being illegal, despite the fact that is defined by the Oxford Dictionary as 'a blackleg; a person who refuses to join a strike or who takes over the work of a striker.' One judge – obviously a man who lived in another world – suggested that pickets should shout *Bounder*, as an alternative! Tony Benn sent me part of his diaries, in which he recorded a meeting with the chief constable of Avon. During the conversation, the chief constable kept referring to the strikers and the scabs, and Tony noted that the use of the latter word on a picket line was an arrestable offence.

Keith Mellin also recalled the early morning trips to picket at Rawdon and its neighbouring pit. "I remember going over to Rawdon and Donisthorpe to picket at four o'clock in the morning, trying to catch the early shift coming in. Three of us, in an Austin 1100, going over in the early hours of the morning. Freezing cold. Sitting there waiting for the day shift to come on. Half an hour and it was all over, they'd all gone in. There were support groups that came as well, outside the pit and stood there. We weren't rowdy or anything, we tried to give out leaflets to anybody that stopped. I remember being at Rawdon, twenty, thirty of us, mostly the support group, and then the police came down the road – about ten of them – and arrested half a dozen people. For whatever. Being disorderly. We hadn't been doing anything. I think it was just a case of getting the figures up. There was a court appearance in Coalville. I remember Billy Scott, he got pulled in. It was all ridiculous. It was out of order, it was all wrong. We had a few laughs though. I remember the heater in my car wasn't working as we were going back and forth to Rawdon, so I got a little stove, and lit it in the car – a really dangerous thing to do."

Although the Dirty Thirty welcomed all help from their families and supporters, Mel Elcock had to ban his father from the picket line for getting too angry with the Leicestershire scabs. "My grandfather was in the 1926 strike. He was also in the First World War – he didn't have to go, he volunteered. Then he went back in the pits. My father spent time on the picket line in 1984. In fact, a policeman escorted him off the car park at Bagworth pit, because he was threatening people with a steel bar. Unfortunately then I had to ban him from the picket lines because he was the sort of chap who couldn't believe what he was seeing. In fifty years or more, he'd never seen people crossing picket lines. There's always been disputes in individual pits, but when that pit went home, everyone went home. My father couldn't believe it. He was asking me, 'What's wrong with these people that they've got no backbone?' Picketing got a bit boring at Bagworth, watching your mates going in, and we knew we weren't going to get any more of them out, so we used to go picketing in South Derbyshire, Nottinghamshire, North Derbyshire, even Yorkshire when Yorkshire cracked, when they started to drift back to work.

"I can remember we were picketing the power station at Ratcliffe on the night the Deputies voted whether to join the strike. We were hoping that they would come out. McGregor even gave them a get-out. He said, 'If you can't cross a picket line with dignity, then you don't have to cross it.' How can you cross a picket line with dignity, there's no such thing. So we thought, That's it, they'll all come out. And then he said, 'We will not close any pits that are viable'. I don't know how many accepted that. If they hadn't believed it, the ballot might have gone in favour of a Deputies' strike. Then when he said about crossing picket lines, I thought that's it. None of them will cross now. But if you remember, Hood, Lynx, and Prendergast – the working miners' leaders – said that they would train their own people to replace any striking Deputies. That would have been illegal, but no doubt the government would have made it legal overnight.

"There was another incident when we were picketing at Ratcliffe. There was a lad called Dave Baker who'd got a Volkswagen and there was six in it, and they'd gone first. When we got there, six policemen had got them all at the side of the van, with their hands on the van, frisking them. We polled

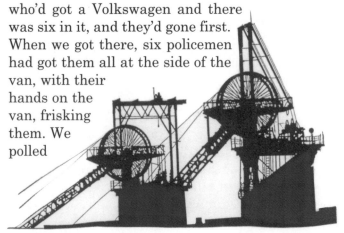

up, there were about eight of us, and they must have thought we were going to attack them. We stopped and said, 'What's the problem?' They said, 'No problem. Somebody has been throwing stones at the train drivers.' 'Well, who's been throwing stones at the train drivers?' 'We know it's not your lads.' We said, 'Well, we've come to picket.' 'Carry on,' they said, 'if you want to picket the power station, that's your right.' Within ten minutes two riot vans arrived. Full on, they kicked us back out the way. Kicking our ankles, you know what I mean, not swinging kicks, just kicking our ankles so we moved back. By now they outnumbered us about four to one, and they were looking for any excuse to arrest us. And you knew if you got arrested, you were going to get the sack.

"Another occasion we were at Rawdon colliery. McGregor was visiting, so we went there picketing. And it snowed and it snowed and it snowed. We were there early to picket the day shift, so we'd been there for six or eight hours by the time he arrived. We were frozen to the marrow. We looked like snowmen. He drove in to the yard. As he drove into through the pit gate, I just lost my head. I thought, I'm not just going to let him just drive past us as if we're not here. I ran across the road. I don't know what I was going to do, boot the car perhaps, I don't know. But this copper fetched me down half way across the road. He said, 'Give it up, lad. If you don't I'll arrest you. Now come back quietly.' So I count myself very lucky to have got a policeman who'd do that. Any of the others would have arrested me, and I'd have been sacked. My job would have been gone, so I count myself very lucky.

"It was strange, because we had Nottinghamshire police in Leicester and Leicestershire police going to man the picket lines in Nottingham. I reckon they did it so that they got paid for 24 hours a day because they were out of their county. They got paid thousands and thousands of pounds, because they were paid for 24 hours a day. There was a massive marquee just outside Coalville, full of them." I've spoken to many policemen who made an absolute fortune from the overtime being paid during the strike. They will point to their large detached house, or show a photo of them standing by a magnificent car, and admit, 'That was my strike house, this was my strike car.'

It wasn't just the police who were travelling about the country: pickets were doing so too. The difference was that the miners were travelling for principle and the knowledge that they were fighting for a just cause, not for massive wage packets. Many of the Dirty Thirty and their supporters had a number of visiting pickets sleeping in their houses.

Mel Elcock recalled, "We were putting Welsh pickets up in our house, and in our supporters' houses. So we had to collect them all up in the morning to be picketing at the pit before six o'clock. After the first picket we'd go round leafleting, then back to picket the afternoon shift to picket again. They were quite long days."

When, during the strike, Wendy and Nigel Jeffery got a house of their own, it was soon full of pickets. "We got the house round July time, but we'd got no furniture, just a three-piece suite and a mattress that were all given to us, all donated. We had a mattress on the floor and a second-hand three-piece suite. We did have two single beds but the visiting pickets used to have those. The cooker was an old one that the people before had left behind. As soon as we moved in here we said, 'Well look, we've got a four-bedroom house. There's no beds but at least there's carpets on the floor.' The first lot that came were the Durham Mechanics. They brought them over here in a minibus, and they loved it. It was a different set-up from what they'd been used to. When these pickets were staying with us Wendy was working at an insurance brokers in Leicester and I'd be off early in the morning to go picketing. When we came home, there'd be a meal on the table. These Durham Mechanics had made us a slap up meal with the food that we'd got through the donated food parcels. They'd make meals you'd never even dream of with just baked beans, corned beef and a bit of potato. They just took over the kitchen and made meals for about twelve of us.

"When we'd had a meal, it was always a case of off down the pub. I had no money at all, but I never had to put my hand in my pocket with these lads. Because they were organised properly, the Durham area NUM would be paying them strike money. Leicestershire NUM was paying us nothing. They'd come down on a Sunday night or sometimes Monday, and then go back on the Friday. On a Monday Tuesday Wednesday, there were never many people in the village pubs, and these were twelve lads from the North-East who liked a drink, plus me and Wendy. They'd fill a place, and they'd be spending money. Even though there was never any trouble, there was one pub in Barlestone – the Lion – who told them that they weren't welcome.

They'd had complaints from the scab miners. I think the scabs were embarrassed by the fact that they were working, and they'd obviously complained to the landlord. We'd gone in this particular day, and the pub was more or less empty, but he didn't want his scab regulars being upset, so we were asked to leave. Then we ended up at the Tuns regular. That was run by an oldish couple, Nancy and Lenny, and they absolutely loved these Durham Mechanics. They used to put sandwiches on for them every night, free of charge. There'd be darts tournaments amongst themselves – and the occasional lock-in. We had some good times with them."

# Demonstrations and Rallies

It was quite common for members of the Dirty Thirty to attend rallies and demonstrations, but they were often events that were heavily and violently policed. Dave Douglas told me about a rally held in London when he had some trouble. "I was only arrested once, and that was in London. My wife Kath was with me. It was supposed to have been an attempted assault on a police officer, but it was because I jumped to my feet too quick. On Horse Guards Parade there was a corner, and across the corner there was a rail that stood about three foot high. There was trouble at Trafalgar Square, and the crowd had backed up all the way past Horse Guards Parade. Nobody was moving, so people started to sit down. The next thing I knew, the gate into Horse Guards Parade opened up, and the horses came out, the police with sticks. It didn't matter if it was a woman or a child, they got clobbered with the long sticks. They were just hitting everybody. So I got Kath – she'd never been on a demonstration, she didn't know what to expect – and I shoved her behind this bit of rail on the corner so that she wouldn't get crushed. I climbed up and stood on top of a bit of fencing, which took me about three foot higher. There was a pushbike chained to it. I stood there to see what was going off, and this copper came along and he said, 'Down.' I hesitated to put my feet on this pushbike to jump down, so he got me by the scruff of my neck and threw me to the floor. As I hit the floor, I heard my wife screaming, and I thought they were dragging her over the fence. I thought he was hurting her so I jumped to my feet. I didn't move towards him or anything, but the next thing I knew I was on my back, with one copper on each arm, one on each leg. They picked me up and carried me off. They just lifted me, carried me off through Horse Guards Parade, chucked me in the back of one of their green wagons that they had round the back. I ended up in Bow Street police station.

"Apparently when Kath asked the police where they were taking me, they wouldn't tell her. Fortunately the support people who were around – not that they knew her – saw that she was upset. They asked her what was the matter and they looked after her. She was in London on her own, because we'd lost contact with the other people we'd gone down with, and there were 50,000 people in the crowd.

"I did make another big mistake. I got invited over to a demonstration in Northern Ireland, by one of the political organisations, the Troops Out Movement. They'd spoken to the NUM, and the NUM agreed for me to go and talk with Sinn Fein on the Belfast radio, about the Troops Out Movement. It was awkward for me because my family was military – I'd got brothers in the army – but I thought I'd go over and see what it was all about. And I took the wife. Big mistake. I should never have taken her, because it was bad enough trying to watch my own back, let alone try to look after her as well. We joined a march against internment down the Falls Road. We were at the front of the march, there were bands playing and it was quite pleasant. Then all of a sudden, everybody had gone, they'd just scattered. The next thing I knew, there was shit happening, rubber bullets and gas flying up the street. I grabbed the wife and chucked her in a doorway. I thought, never again. You want to be able to run without thinking you're responsible for somebody else. I think that was why Malcolm didn't like women on the picket line, because sometimes you were in danger that a copper would hit you. Their shields would cover them down to their knees, so the coppers would kick our shins and ankles. They'd put their shields up, march forward and kick. They'd got steel toe-capped boots."

Mel Elcock told me that the worst incident with police that he can remember was when there was a rally in Mansfield, with thousands of miners there from all over the country. "This bus had got to pick us up to take us back to Loughborough, and this meant we were some of the first to leave. We were heading out of Mansfield to meet the bus, and we saw all the riot vans. We hadn't seen them all day, just one or two policemen, but nobody gave them any trouble and they didn't give us any trouble. We just did the demonstration, and it was finishing. Then they come charging down the road like the Seventh Cavalry. It was unbelievable. What kicked off, what started it, I don't know. We all got in the side. They weren't after us, they were charging into the town centre. They wanted to catch the main body. I saw people afterwards and they told us that the police were pushing people from South Wales onto buses for Scotland, people from Scotland onto buses from Kent. And if they didn't want to get on, they were getting a bit of truncheon and were arrested. Our bus had actually gone without us, so we were all sat on this green mound out of the way. Another riot van came down, stopped, looked at us then drove off again. We'd got women and kids with us, but so had the others."

Commenting on the same rally, Darren Moore said, "I remember in April we went to a Mansfield rally where Arthur Scargill spoke, and where the police waded in after the rally, when most of the miners had gone home. We saw all that. I remember there were miners and supporters from Coventry arrested and charged with riot. Michael Mansfield defended them and they did get found not guilty. The police had waited until people were clearing off and then were going round on horseback whacking people, including school kids, to provoke us. It was disgraceful and opened my eyes to what they were prepared to do."

Going to a rally could be a potentially dangerous and an eye-opening occasion, but it could have its funny moments, too. Sam Girvan recalled, "There was one night when we were going down to Brighton, to a rally, and I picked up young Mick Poli. Now in the back of my car, I'd got my builders tools because I'd been moving a drain. We're going down the M1 and of course the coppers pull us over, because they knew all our registration numbers. 'Where are you going?' Mick Poli gets out and says, 'Fishing.' 'Open your boot.' So I gets out and in the boot I'd got a crowbar and a hook. The copper says, 'What's this for?' I says, 'There's some fucking big fish where we're going!' He says, 'You're going to Brighton.' Of course they knew where we were going, they used to follow us every-where. We were actually going to Northampton to get picked up to go on to Brighton with the support group for the TUC rally. One of the Dirty Thirty, Bob MacSporran, was speaking at the rally. He was the president of the Midlands Area Power Group and a member of the NUM national executive."

Another amusing incident occurred when Margaret and Dennis Thatcher were on a visit to Leicester. Bob Girvan, Mick Poli and other members of the Dirty Thirty went to demonstrate. The public were being held back behind aluminium barriers, and the demonstrators were using a megaphone to shout well deserved 'advice' at the hated Prime Minister. Mick Poli asked to borrow the megaphone, and they were expecting to hear him shout, 'Maggie-Maggie-Maggie, Out-Out-Out,' or perhaps some more original political comment. However, they were demonstrating near St Margaret's bus station, and Bob and the others were somewhat taken aback to hear Mick address a young lady on the upper deck of a passing bus. 'Pretty girl on the bus,' shouted Mick, 'what are you doing on Saturday night?'

On the same occasion, as Bob Girvan was pressing forward on the barrier, he accidentally caused a policeman's helmet to fall off. However he was very lucky because instead of being arrested, thumped or sworn at, Bob was surprised to hear, 'Ey up Bob, how are you doing? How many kids have you got now?' The policeman who'd lost his helmet was a Malc Wilton, a chap Bob had been at school with in Coalville. Bob was fortunate that it was a local policeman, not one of the imported policemen from the Met, keen to show the local Leicestershire miners and the Leicestershire police how tough they were.

# Spreading the Word Further Afield

Some members of the Dirty Thirty travelled much further than County Durham, South Wales and Scotland to spread the word, to tell those who were prepared to listen the story of the Dirty Thirty – to explain what the miners' strike was all about, and to tell the world that there really were miners in Leicestershire with the courage to put their principles before their immediate comfort.

In early 1985, Darren Moore was invited to go and talk about the miners' strike in Italy. "Towards the end of the strike I went to Italy to raise funds. We were there with two left wing groups, Trotskyist groups. They'd had a levy of their members and paid for us to go over to do this speaking tour. I'd been a bit involved with an organisation called Workers Power, and they had links with these Italian groups.

The Italian groups had pooled a levy together to take us over there. There were three of us: me, a miner from Yorkshire, Pete – he worked at Brodsworth pit near Doncaster – and a lad from South Wales. We started off in Rome speaking at the university, where someone told us the political police were in the audience. I did not realise who they were at the time. We also did a phone in on an anarchist radio station where we got all sorts of questions. I was in Rome for three days before I went to Umbria, staying with this guy's parents. Although they were well to do and owned a hotel, they were members of the Communist Party. This guy was a chef and he worked in the family hotel. We stayed in the hotel and he cooked for us. One day he took us to see a veteran anti-fascist who opened his best twenty-year-old wine for us.

"Later on, I remember speaking in a small town in Umbria. I was speaking in the Town Hall, and there was a big red flag flying in the town square. We went into the meeting, and saw this guy sitting at the back. He had a leather jacket on, and a thin leather tie. He was chewing gum, and he had this slicked back hair, just how you imagine someone from the mafia to look like. He just looked like a stereotype. I said, 'Who's that?' because he didn't look like one of the normal people who came to the meetings, students or some of the left wing crowd. We had translators who told us, 'Oh, he's from the political police.' He was sitting there with his notepad, writing everything down we said. I thought that he was trying to intimidate us. After the meeting, he came up and asked for our passports in a really heavy-handed way. It was like one of these scenes you see in a B movie. He was looking at our passports, looking at us, then writing things down. He wasn't asking any questions, just chewing his gum. I thought, this has got to be a joke. At the time the Red Brigades were operating in Italy, so the authorities had clamped down, like today with terrorism. Some of the liberties we're losing now are because of the threat of terrorism. That's what was happening in Italy then.

"This guy even followed us back to the car. He kept looking in the shop windows, and as soon as we went past, he followed us. We said to the translator, 'There he is again.' On the way back to the car, he was looking at his paper and following us. He wasn't even doing it very well. It was exactly like a Peter Sellers' film. When we got back to the car, he did come up and ask the people who we were with for their ID cards because you had to carry them in Italy back then, something they are trying to bring in here now. We were told that people in left wing political groups used to get harassed all the time. They told me that their office got turned over in the night and a lot of their stuff was chucked on the floor.

"I had to laugh at one meeting, when this girl got up and what she said caused uproar. I asked what she'd said and the translator said, 'She's saying that all the Communist officials want to do is fuck young girls.' There was obviously a bit of corruption going on in the area.

"We went all round. We went to Turin, Genoa and Milan. Turin was very interesting because they'd got a curfew in the evening on the streets, because of the Red Brigades. The big Fiat car factory is there and at the meeting I was talking about police brutality, and saying, 'The police are battering the miners.' One of the big convenors from the Fiat plant asked me, 'Well, what do you expect?' I thought he had a point. If you set yourself up against the state, and the state's under threat from what you're doing, then they are going to use everything at their disposal to put you down. When they have a strike in Italy it often gets explosive and they do set up the barricades, but it was a relative rare occurrence in UK industrial disputes.

"There aren't really any mines in Italy but they were very interested in the political aspect. I'd just finished our speaking tour, and this guy from the Communist Party came up and said, 'I want you to come back. We'll pay for you to come back for two weeks and go round some of our workers' meetings and tell them about the miners' strike.' When I came back from Italy, Benny picked me up. I was full of beans and said, 'Benny, they want us to go back, and they'll help us raise some more money and they'll pay for everything.' Benny said, 'Hang on, Darren. The strike will be over on Monday. They've got a meeting down in London to decide whether to continue the strike, and it looks like it's going to be called off.' This took the wind right out of my sails because I was ready for another year on strike. I went down to that meeting and it was when it was decided to end the strike, it was an anticlimax for me, to be defeated after all the hard work we had put in. I'd just come back on a high and now it was all over, the strike was called off. The worst thing was that there were a lot of miners who had either been sacked or they were in prison and who couldn't go back to work, including people we knew like Wardy and Jim Quinn from Coventry pit and Tony Clegg from Doncaster."

A few months after the strike was over, other members of the Dirty Thirty travelled to the USA. Richo Richmond told me, "We'd met these American people down in London, and eventually out of the blue, they said, 'We'd like you to come to Oberlin

College in Ohio.' They paid for everything. Not everybody could go, and Benny didn't want to go, but a group of us went. We flew across to New York – JFK airport. I never thought I'd see that, never in my life. I even took some photos from the twin towers."

Nigel Jeffery recalled, "My dad went, Richo, Dave Douglas, Bunny Warren, Phil Smith and myself. We were invited out to this Oberlin College outside of Cleveland in Ohio. At the time, I'd never even been on a plane before. It was a different world over there. I'd seen America on the films, and now we were there. At first, we were put up in New Jersey, and we used to travel into New York, Manhattan, up the World Trade Centre. We never actually met the people who put us up. We were put up in these apartments, and the people were literally gone in the morning. They went to work at seven in the

*The Dirty Thirty in New York 1985.*

morning. We'd wake up at nine. And at night, we had a key to let ourselves in, being as quiet as we could, and they'd be in bed. They were very hospitable.

"I did the Manhattan cruise with my dad, round the Hudson River – that was an experience. It was then that we heard about baseball. Even though my dad had never been into sport – I was always the sporty one – we decided to go to the Yankee Stadium in the middle of the Bronx. Bunny went with us as well. The baseball started in the afternoon and it was what they called a double-header. Because I know baseball now, I realise it must have been that they had backlogs of games, so they'd bring two together, an afternoon game and then straight into a night game. We got on the Metro from where we were stopping, the subway train, we got on in New Jersey and rode straight out to the stadium. Well, this second game kept going and we were thinking we should be getting back. It started to get dark, and we left the second game half way through, because we were thinking of the time. It was about nine, ten o'clock. It's scary enough in the daytime. It was one of the scariest experiences of my life, riding the tube at night, going from the Bronx back to New Jersey. It was exactly what you see on the films. These tubes were covered in graffiti, inside and out, and there were gangs patrolling about. These youths – black, white, Hispanic – were walking up and down these trains as though they were looking to mug somebody. We were sitting there wetting ourselves. We hadn't been expecting this. It was completely alien to me and to my dad. My dad says, 'Don't look at them, just look down at the floor or out the window.' We were relieved when we got off at New Jersey, but even then it weren't finished. We still had to come out of the subway, and you didn't feel secure. There was a lot of unrest. In the background we could hear sirens going. I remember, as we came out of that subway, me, my dad and Bunny, we'd gone across the road into a bar. And while we were there, we heard guns going off – somebody had been shot across the road. We watched out of this bar window, as the ambulances and police came screaming. It was like being in a film set."

Phil Smith's main memory of the stay in New York was of the generosity of their hosts. "When we got off the plane, this lady met us and said she'd take us to where we were stopping. We were all stopping in different places. I went up this block of flats with her and she said, 'Right, here's the key. Let yourself in.' When I asked her where the people who lived there were, she said, 'They're not in.

*Nigel and Cliff Jeffery in USA 1985, joining an American union picket line.*

They're away.' I said, 'I can't go in there if they're away.' She said, 'Yes, you can. Here's your key.' It was a lovely flat, absolutely terrific. I thought, I can't believe this. They don't know me from Adam and I'm in their flat. I went in the kitchen, and found a notepad there, which said, 'Hi Phil. We'll probably not get to meet you, which will be a disappointment. But this flat is yours for as long as you want it.' We were thousands of miles away from home, and they were so incredibly generous."

The Leicestershire miners then travelled to Oberlin by Greyhound bus. According to Nigel, Oberlin itself was built round a crossroads. He recalled, "Again it was like something you might see on the films. You could see the four roads for miles in each direction, and all the shops, the bars and the restaurants were at these crossroads."

At the college, set outside of the town, the Dirty Thirty men used to meet people and run a stall during the day, and attend meetings in the evenings. There were people there from all over the world, ANC activists from South Africa, Sandinistas from Nicaragua, and of course members of the Dirty Thirty. Richo told me that at one meeting, he was sitting next to Oliver Tambo. "Have you heard of Oliver Tambo from the ANC? Well, he was next to me on this platform. Here's me a miner from Ibstock and here's Nelson Mandela's right hand man sat next to me. I looked round and thought, What am I doing here? We were all supporting each other, the anti-apartheid people, the striking miners, the Sandinistas from Nicaragua. The chairman of the meeting was a huge black man, an American socialist called Malik Miah. There were about two thousand people in the corrugated roofed arena, open-sided. Malik Miah opened the rally, and I thought, Why are they all clapping? But it wasn't clapping, it was the rain on the corrugated roof. You can tell how vast the place was, because it was thunderous. I started laughing, and I looked at Oliver Tambo and he said, 'You thought they were clapping. So did I.' The chairman, Malik, stopped the meeting and said, 'Hang on. Richo is laughing about something. What are you laughing at?' I explained that I'd thought people were applauding but it was in fact the rain. The whole place went into uproar, and then they did start clapping."

Richo also recalled one of his most embarrassing moments. "We did a number of different workshops, and they were asking about life down the pits. Towards the end, when we'd been there about a week, we were all on this stage and there were about five hundred people out in front. We were all crapping ourselves, but we all did our share of speaking: Phil Smith, Nigel Jeffrey, Bunny Warren. Then I had to do the last question and answer session, and this woman got up and she asked me, as I heard it, about what I thought about the Gays and the Lesbians. I was going on and on, saying that I wasn't bothered whether they were gay or lesbian, they were supporters and they were just fantastic people. After the meeting, she came up to me and she said, 'I asked you about the gains and lessons that had been learned from the strike.' I said, 'You're joking!' I died a death there on the spot. She'd said gains and lessons and I'd heard Gays and Lesbians.

"On the final night – they call it the closing rally night – I sat on this top forum. I did a speech, giving greetings from the NUM, greetings from Leicester-shire, and then I said, 'I can't bring any greetings from the scabs.' And that brought the house down. It broke me up a bit, because I was so angry."

One family had the opportunity to visit East Germany after the strike. The miners from that country had invited one family from each mining area to go there on a holiday, and the Women's Group decided that it should be Cliff Jeffery's wife and children. That family had given so much to the strike; Cliff himself was on strike, as were his son Nigel and his stepson's Mark and Alan.

Barbara Jeffery told me, "In July 1985, my daughter Lynn, my young son Dean and myself were invited to visit East Germany. The offer came from the East German miners' union. At that time most of the Dirty Thirty wives were working or had other commitments, but my husband insisted that it was too good an opportunity to miss, so I accepted the invitation. Along with striking miners' wives from other areas, we were transported to Leeds-Bradford airport and we boarded an Aeroflot airliner and flown to Erfurt. Upon landing, we were warmly greeted by union members, a brass band playing in the background, and each of us were given a rose and toys for the children. From there we were taken to Schmiedefeld and put up in a lovely new hotel for the following fortnight. During our stay, we were taken on several outings to interesting places. Our first outing was to Oberhof winter sports centre. We walked through a forest and then back down at the side of the bobsleigh run. Another trip was to Buchenwald, the infamous prison camp. It was grim and upsetting to see where the prisoners were tortured and to see the ovens where the bodies were burnt. The children were not allowed on the camp visit and were taken to a toy museum instead. A visit to a salt mine one day ended with a banquet where food and wine was abundant. Two days before we were due to fly home, we were taken into town to a big store where we could get presents for our family back home. All the presents we received – including new coats and jumpers – were free. It was a great experience, and we were very grateful to the then East German miners' union."

# Going Back to Work

In many mining areas the return to work, after the strike was called off in March 1985, was conducted with the men marching back proudly behind their union banners. In Leicestershire it was less ceremonial. Malcolm Pinnegar told me, "It was not easy for us to go back down Bagworth pit with men who regarded us as the enemy." Richo recalled, "Although in most areas, the NUM marched back to work with bands, and with their heads held high, we just turned up and walked in. I felt desolate, physically  sick. Some people spoke to us, others didn't. I just eyeballed them. There was a hell of an atmosphere." Darren Moore added, "My stomach dropped when we all sat in the canteen at Bagworth waiting to see the manager to sort out returning to work, but at least my conscience was clear and I could hold my head high."

Actually the return of some of the Bagworth men was held up for a week by a claim from Jack Jones, the general secretary of the Leicestershire NUM, that the men were no longer paid-up members of the union. However once that was sorted, they went back to work. Malcolm commented, "We were lucky at Bagworth, because the manager and one of his

Deputies were very fair and stamped down on any intimidation." The manager concerned was Mr Bond, who according to Darren Moore, had been a miner who had worked his way up to pit manager. Although he didn't like Arthur Scargill and he wasn't in favour of the strike, he was a pitman first and foremost, so he had some respect for those men who had been fighting to save the pits.

A meeting was held by Mr Bond, an under-manager and the Bagworth striking miners, together with Trevor Hines and Pat Callaghan, respectively delegates for the colliers and the power group – but both men who had worked during the strike. Mr Bond asked Malcolm to open the meeting, and he told the manager, "We know that we lost the strike but we all believe what we did was right. We know that we cannot dictate what happens to us, but I ask you not to make the same mistake that you did when you wrote a letter of support to the court for the scab who threatened my daughter and came looking for trouble to my house at two o'clock in the morning. You also allowed a collection at the pit to pay his fine, and you know I'm telling the truth."

Malcolm tells me that the manager was shocked, his first reaction being to tell Malcolm that he couldn't call anyone a scab if they were to get back to normal working. As the meeting progressed Malcolm could see that his outburst had worked, and Mr Bond was prepared to put the strikers back to work in groups, not as individuals. Everything was sorted until Malcolm asked the two delegates whether they would receive full and fair representation from the local union on resumption of work underground. Pat Callaghan said the fitters and electricians would have no problems and would be fully represented – which was no surprise as Bob McSporran, the power group area president was a member of the Dirty Thirty. However, when Trevor Hines was asked, he refused to give the same assurance, which meant that the men could not resume work. Malcolm told me, "Mr Bond was visibly annoyed with Hines and told him to get the matter sorted, and if he couldn't, to find someone who could. Hines left the meeting to ring Jack Jones, just like he had at the beginning of the strike, but didn't return to the meeting."

The fitters and electricians returned to work but the colliers were unable to as they were still not represented. It was to take a whole week and intervention by the national NUM before the situation was resolved.

Mel Elcock had met with the manager a week earlier, as the power workers – the electricians and fitters – hadn't had the same trouble with their NUM membership being queried. Mel said, "Mr Bond was from the North-East, you see, a Geordie. He said he was glad to have us all back, he admired us. I don't know what he thought about the people who'd worked, but he said he admired us." Mel didn't actually want to go back before Benny, Richo and the others, out of a feeling of solidarity. "I decided to stay out with the other lads, the non power-group lads. I decided that I'd been on strike for a year, and I'd go back when the others went back. However, the next day, Bob McSporran told him, 'Mel, you're not in dispute any more. If you don't go back, they can judge you as being absent.

111

You have to go back.' So I explained to the lads that I had to go back. There was no problem with them, obviously. We were all mates."

Darren told me that the manager put a group of the Dirty Thirty together for the first few weeks on a coalface, salvaging. "I suppose in a way it was in his best interest, because he didn't want any trouble or violence from the majority who'd worked. He didn't have to do that, he could have made it tough for us. Benny knew Bondy, and he always got on with him because he called a spade a spade." Later Darren worked in a team with Benny and Dave Douglas driving tunnels, or heading. "Some of the scabs were fine, no problems, but others wouldn't talk to us at first. They were very antagonistic as if it was them who'd lost a year's pay. Others did say, 'We should have been out,' usually using the excuse of the absence of a national ballot. Some of them had been on strike for a short time. There were seventy or eighty men out for a few days until Jack Jones and Trevor Hines scuppered it with the local ballot. We were all strong willed, especially after a year on strike, so our point of view would be unwavering. When we went on heading, we were on piecework so we had to graft but we had to take all sorts of risks and that's one of the problems with the bonus scheme."

Malcolm, Darren and Dave made a formidable team. They had kept the solidarity, the comradeship, forged in the year on strike together and they brought it back to work with them. Darren recalled how they'd used it to defeat a Deputy who hated the Dirty Thirty and was deliberately causing them grief. "I remember we had one Deputy who was renowned down the pit for being power crazy. He was put in charge of me, Benny and Dave. He did a number of things to us. We had been getting water money [extra money because of wet conditions] but he stopped that. Another thing he did, he told us to bring the machine back and clean the floor. Benny told him to eff off. At the end of a shift he told us to put the air trowin [plastic air pipes] in. It was his responsibility but he'd been happy for us to cut coal all day with no air, breathing in all the dust with the air trowin right back. Then he wanted us to do it when the shift was finished. Again we told him to eff off. He went and wrote a report for the manager, saying that we had told him to eff off."

According to Dave Douglas, Benny's approach was to give the man a load of lip, but Darren had a better way of dealing with him. Darren explained, "He used to get off on power, that was his problem. He was one of these people who liked to be in charge and to show you who's the boss, so he liked it when he got people riled. We decided to send him to Coventry. Benny says, 'I don't know about that. I don't know if I can keep quiet.' Dave Douglas was a bit like me so I knew he wouldn't have any problem with it. So the Deputy comes down at the beginning of the shift and he says, 'I want you to do this, I want you to do that.' We just ignored him, we just kept talking to each other, just ignoring what he said. You could see he was looking a bit bemused. He said, 'Well, I take it you've got that then.' So he went off. Obviously we knew how to do the job, so we didn't really need a Deputy to tell us anything. After two days the undermanager come down. He says, 'You can't go on like this.' We said, 'Well, we've not got a problem. The job's getting done.

What's the problem? He's just trying to show us he's boss. There's no need. We can do the job just as well without any help from him, so until he apologises, we're not going to communicate with him.' Well, a day later he came down and apologised – he almost broke down. Basically we'd taken his power away, and that was the only thing he craved. It was amazing really. In two days he was almost a broken man. A day later, they put him with another gang and he was soon messing them about and being difficult with them. We got somebody else who was fine. With coming out on strike, we knew we could stick together and win a few battles." Obviously this heading team – Malcolm, Dave and Darren – was not a group to tangle with!

Dave Douglas was even more chipper, and enjoyed winding up the scabs. "I used to take the piss. I weren't bothered. They were never going to get the better of me, they were never going to break me even though they broke the strike. Because it was the scabs that broke the strike. They used to blame the national ballot – but even if we'd had one, they'd have still worked. At the end of the day there were 140,000 miners out on strike. What did you need a ballot for? They'd walked out, voted with their feet. Down the pit, there are three buttons on a tannoy system. I used to press the Speak button and sing songs to them. I used to say, 'Come in, scabs.'

That song I used to sing to them down the pit started:

*In nineteen hundred and eighty four, shit really hit the fan*
*When Mack the knife McGregor, Maggie Thatcher's hatchet man,*
*Said another forty pits will have to close to meet the plan.*
*And we'll dump another forty thousand miners.*

The chorus was:

*Daddy, what did you do in the strike?*
*Did you stand upon the picket line and fight?*
*Or did you show your lily-liver,*
*Sell your union down the river,*
*Daddy what did you do in the strike?*

"There were lots more verses to it, but it was the chorus that I liked to sing over the tannoy. It was a well known song during the strike. I used to say, 'I'm going to come round when you're buried and write SCAB on your tombstone.' I got told off by this undermanager, Mr Fergusson. He said, 'Dave, you can't be calling them scabs over the tannoy system. You've got to think of something else.' I said that I couldn't think of anything else, and he suggested Henry. He said, 'Call them Henries.' And that was what they got for the rest of my time down the pit. I used to go on the tannoy system, saying, 'Come in Henry.' To me it was just another name for a scab.

"I dug a grave once. We were clearing this area, salvaging. There was a water pool we were digging out, about two foot wide and six foot long, two foot deep. It looked just like a grave to me. I got a bit of wood together and I wrote on it *R.I.P. Henry*, and stuck it at the end of this hole. I sat there next to it, watching them all go by. Everybody was looking at it and then looking away. Benny was in hysterics, he was having kittens, wetting himself.

"The thing was, the scabs hadn't got anything to argue with us. At the end of the day, they hadn't got an argument. Their jobs were in jeopardy because we'd lost the strike and that was down to them. They'd sold their own jobs down the river. They

115

hadn't got an argument so they never did confront us. They only thing they said was – and this was annoying – 'Yeah, we should have been out there with you.' Personally, I wouldn't have crossed the picket line if I were the only one not to. I'd have probably have got the sack but it wouldn't have mattered. I just wouldn't do it."

Malcolm told me that over the next couple of years his faith in the manager, Mr Bond, was fully restored. "When any incidents involving any member of the Dirty Thirty occurred – and there were quite a few – I would be fetched out of the pit by the manager, and we would sort it out between us, without the involvement of Hines and his cronies. The Dirty Thirty lads at Bagworth acknowledge that Mr Bond behaved like a proper man and he was respected by all the strikers."

Mick Richmond – Richo – didn't find the atmosphere at Bagworth as easy as Benny, Darren and Dave. "We got a letter, Phil Smith, Sammy Girvan, Mick Barnes and me, summoning us to one of the undermanagers. He said, 'Er, it's not a punishment but we've got to be seen to be doing something. So we're going to send you on nights to clean out the drifts at Nailstone.' Now it was cold and wet, but we were on regular nights, so we were getting 50% more wages than we were at Bagworth, and we were getting 100% bonus. We were stacks better off. We were just wandering round Nailstone drift telling jokes most nights, and laughing us heads off. And that was deemed as a punishment. We had three months there, before he finally dropped on that it wasn't a punishment at all, we were just making money for nothing. It was brilliant. We used to sit

116

under the main drift belt that was whizzing over us heads, bringing the coal out from Bagworth. And we just sat, getting paid. All we had to do was clean the spillage up, coal that came off the belts. Three of us, all face trained. We'd start at the top and come to the bottom, then we'd come back up and start again. We loved it. And that was a punishment? Whatever."

Richo obviously interpreted the comment 'This is not a punishment but ...' as an unmistakable sign that their deployment at Nailstone *was* a punishment. I asked Sammy Girvan what he thought. Sam laughed and said, "After the dispute, we got a bit of hassle and Richo, Mick Barnes, Phil Smith and myself, we ended up working at Nailstone, on the drift. It was wet and rainy, horrible. I don't know if it was meant as a punishment but what was a bit of a punishment for me was having to work with Richo and Mick Barnes, because they would argue relentlessly, all the time. Phil Smith's a bit of a mickey-taker so Phil and I used to wind them up, and get them arguing. Just for the sake of it."

Mel Elcock recalled, "I went back and I was greeted by the mechanical engineer, who that day wanted to meet the four power group lads who'd been on strike. We had a meeting with him. He'd come to Bagworth pit during the strike. He was very good to us. He interviewed us, he told us if there were any problems to take them to him, and he would sort it out. He said he understood why we'd done what we'd done, and there'd be no problems from him. I went to the deployment office, and the deputy engineers and the assistant engineers all shook my hand. I went down to the workshop, which

117

near enough came to a standstill when they seen me walking in. I said, 'Where's my band?' and everybody laughed. There was no hostility from any craftsmen as we called them, the electrical and mechanical workers. I had no problem with any of them.

"I went back to work on a face. I had no problems there, but then I was put on an installation face. These were some of the people who we knew we would have trouble with. When I went to work on this face there was about 50% of them wouldn't speak to me. This was no hardship for me; I just did my job. After about a fortnight, every one of them except one was speaking to me. That really put me in charge, because this man expected everybody to stand by him, but they knew me – I went to work, I did my job, I'm a friendly guy in the main. They were wrong, I was right, they knew it and I knew it. This guy didn't speak to me and I didn't speak to him, that's how it finished up "

Bob Girvan had some stick when he first went back. "When we went down, all the day shift were waiting to go out, and they were all shouting, 'Scab! Scab!' at us." A number of the Dirty Thirty mentioned how bizarre it was when the scabs, the working miners, used to call the strikers scabs. Perhaps they thought it was just another word for a minority. Maybe it was because the Dirty Thirty ignored what they regarded as an irrelevant and unnecessary local ballot. Whatever the reason, they'd got it wrong. The dictionary definition of a scab as a worker who works during a strike is very clear. Bob continued, "We walked straight through, staring at 'em, and they parted and let us through.

And as they let us through, they all started shouting 'scab' again, and that was our first day back down the pit." Bob recalled a later occasion when a bloke mumbled something about the Dirty Thirty being scabs as he walked past. Bob says that he had to stop young Mick Barnes from getting up and doing something about it, because he didn't want Mick to get the sack.

Keith Mellin was an electrician at Ellistown where only four miners had joined the strike. He told me, "Actually they weren't too bad. I had a few comments, I suppose. In fact there was one bloke who gave me a bit of verbal, but nothing too bad." At South, Johnny Gamble was the only man to strike, but he too said, "I only ever had one problem at South, just one bloke who refused to work with me. I said, 'Fine. I didn't particularly want to work with you either.' And that was it. Then within a week I was on a permanent heading team." I think all the miners, even the more extreme of the scabs, recognised the courage of a man who had come out on strike on his own. Richo commented, "In all the pits, there was a lot of animosity from the other miners. But the one man from South who joined the Dirty Thirty, Johnny Gamble, he was really respected for what he did."

# "The Good, the Bad and the Ugly"

In Malcolm's view, there were three types of people who interacted with the Dirty Thirty: the good, the bad and the ugly. In the first group, he puts the wives and families, who put up with a year of hardship, never wavering in their support for their husbands, sons and brothers. He also has overwhelming admiration for the Mantle Lane railwaymen who blacked any movement of Leicestershire coal by train. Every one of the Dirty Thirty I talked to spoke with gratitude and appreciation about the railwaymen. Bob Girvan said, "We've got to remember the Coalville railwaymen who put their jobs on the line for us. They were fantastic." Richo's comment was, "Round here in Coalville, the railwaymen were heroes, absolute heroes." Also among the *good* were the support groups in Leicester, Loughborough, Coalville and beyond, and everyone who donated money and food to the cause.

Malcolm also acknowledges the help given to the Dirty Thirty by the national officers of the NUM, particularly the president and general secretary. "Arthur Scargill and Peter Heathfield never let us down, and considering their national responsibilities, this was no mean feat. Peter Heathfield was held in the highest regard by all members of the Dirty Thirty. The Dirty Thirty were able to use the national NUM solicitors in all local court cases with all costs covered by the national union, and the national union covered the enormous phone bills incurred by the Dirty Thirty leaders."

In the *bad* category, Malcolm would include the scabs, the miners who worked throughout the strike, the miners who allowed the government to proceed with their plans to shut down the coal industry. I think he would also include the police, particularly the imported police from the Met and elsewhere, who allowed themselves to be manipulated into taking a partisan role against the strikers.

He saves the word *ugly* for those people who actively sought to undermine the Dirty Thirty. First and foremost among these was Jack Jones, the secretary of the Leicestershire NUM, a member of the minority delegates at the National Executive, and a determined opponent of the strike. When the Kent

*The Dirty Thirty meet Peter Heathfield, NUM General Secretary.*
*Back row: Andrew Findell, Cliff Jeffery, Billy Scott, Nigel*
*Jeffery, Wendy Jeffery.*
*Front row: Mark Findell, Sam Girran, Peter Heathfield and*
*Bob Girvan.*

pickets first came to Leicestershire, they were allowed to address a canteen meeting in Bagworth colliery, and the eighty miners present agreed to support the strike, as mentioned earlier. When Jack Jones heard about this he was furious and, fearing a build-up of pro-strike impetus, he ordered the men to return to work. Faced with this division in the advice from different parts of the union, most of the men did as Jack Jones had instructed.

When the few remaining strikers and their supporters began to picket the local pits, Jack Jones issued that statement in the local press, declaring that he would lead his members through the picket lines, carrying a baseball bat if necessary. This threat of potential violence came, it should be noted, from a vehement opponent of the strike, not from the strikers.

Another clash with the Dirty Thirty came when Jack banned the striking miners from attending union meetings. Mick Richmond asked me, "Did you know that me and Benny took him to the High Court, because they prevented us from speaking at union branch meetings during the strike? We were fully paid-up members, and they kept banning us from meetings so in the end we took legal advice. Supporters of the strike all over the country, all over the world, were helping us and put us in touch with Siefert Sedley Williams, big lawyers down in London. We'd threatened to take Jack Jones to court, and he attended a Bagworth meeting and said, 'The Dirty Thirty are bluffing. They will not do it.' But we did, we took them to the High Court and the court found in our favour. We had to go round different lodge members and serve the summons on

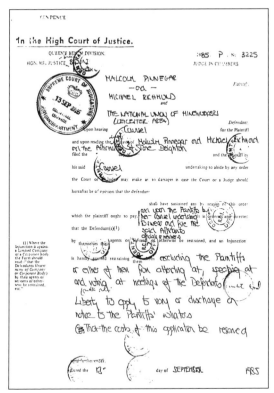

*Material relating to successful action taken by the Dirty Thirty leaders at the High Court to compel Leicestershire Area NUM to allow Dirty Thirty to attend and speak at local NUM meetings.*

them. I went up Greenhill Road to Jack Jones's house, and he says, 'Hello, Mick.' I says, 'I should read that, me duck, if I were you.' He said, 'What is it?' I said, 'It's what you read out at the meeting.' He said, 'You silly man.' I said, 'Well, I'll be able to speak now at the next meeting unless you dare flout it.' And he daren't. He couldn't disobey the court order. It was one of the best moments of the strike.

At the very next union meeting, it was Benny who said, 'Before you start, read that out.' Jack Jones was spluttering, he really was. He says, 'These people have cost Leicestershire NUM five thousand pounds, in court costs.' And I said, 'Well, we did tell you, Jack.'"

When the strike ended, Jack Jones attempted to stop the Dirty Thirty from going back to their jobs in the Leicestershire pits, again arguing that they were not paid-up members of the NUM. Mel Elcock explained, "There had been complications with our union membership. Scargill had waived the membership dues for all the miners who were on strike, but Leicestershire NUM had said, "We're working so you do have to pay."

Darren Moore gave me further details. "We found out the Leicestershire NUM were trying to stop us going back to work and we could not go back underground without union representation in case of accidents. So we could not go back until it was sorted out. It was different for the craftsmen, electricians and fitters like Mel, Bunny and Chissy because they were in the Power Group which had no problems with them returning. We had to get the national union involved to challenge the Leicestershire area union. We had always argued that the national union rulebook takes precedence over the local rulebook – because the NUM was federated, each area had its own rule book as well as a national one – and this was part of the reason we were on strike. It had taken an extra week but we could now return to work. The issue for me was that the union delegates and Jack Jones of Leicestershire NUM had tried to humiliate us and had failed."

On one occasion during the strike Benny and Richo – Malcolm Pinnegar and Mick Richmond – got a tip-off that there was a breakaway trade union being formed, and a meeting was being held at the Brant Hotel in Groby. Richo told me, "We followed them and they were all there, Jack Jones from Leicestershire, Horace Sankey and Ken Toon from South Derbyshire, plus the UDM [Union of Democratic Miners, the breakaway union] people from Nottinghamshire, all of them. And the same night, the very same night, Jack Jones publicly denied that he'd ever been to the place. And yet we saw him there, we saw them all there."

Mention of the formation of the UDM leads to Terry Hughes, another man who Benny regards as one of the *ugly*. The UDM was formed by the miners who had scabbed in Nottinghamshire. Notts miners had a tradition of forming breakaway right-wing unions when they had been through a strike. In 1926 remember, following the miners' strike, they formed the Spencer union. In 1985 they formed the UDM. South Derbyshire decided to transfer from the NUM to the UDM by the narrowest of margins, a mere 16 votes.

There were those, Terry Hughes among them, who wanted to see Leicestershire do the same. Mel Elcock told me, "There was really what you might call a domino effect. Obviously it started in Nottinghamshire, it had rolled through South Derbyshire and the idea was it'd roll through Leicestershire. There was this guy called Terry Hughes, a delegate from Ellistown, he organised a meeting at St Wilfred's Club in Coalville with an attempt to persuade everybody in the Leicestershire coalfield to join the UDM. He invited Neil Greatrex from Nottinghamshire and Ken Toon from South Derbyshire to be on the platform, and there was an open invitation to all Leicestershire miners.

"I spoke to Gordon Smith and he said, 'Are we going to go over and participate in the meeting?' In a proper manner, obviously. There were about five of us went. We got together and decided what questions we were going to fire at who. We sat at different places round the hall, so they couldn't spot us as a group. They made a bit of a speech about the UDM and how they saw democracy. They asked for questions and I directed my question at Ken Toon. I said, 'You're condemning Arthur Scargill and the national NUM rulebook. Can you explain to me, Ken, that you've had a rulebook in South Derbyshire for probably fifty years and it's been good enough for you for that length of time. And in that rulebook it says that you've got to have four-fifths of the membership to dissolve the South Derbyshire NUM. Now when Scargill changed it to a simple majority rule, you condemned him and said you should stick by the original rules. So can you tell me at what time and what date you changed your mind about your own rulebook?' Because South Derbyshire had voted by a tiny majority to join the UDM. He went red – he looked like he was going to have a heart attack – and he blustered it out. He said, 'Well, if you come to see me after the meeting, I'll explain.' I said, 'I don't want to come and see you after the meeting, Ken, I want you to explain to everybody here how you stand on rulebooks. Is it a simple majority, or is it the rulebook you've had for fifty odd years, saying that there's got to be four-fifths? Where do you stand?' And he didn't say anything, because Terry Hughes said, 'Are there any more questions?'

"Then Gordon Smith asked a question, and every hand up was a member of the Dirty Thirty. There must have been other NUM members there but they didn't put their hands up. Hughes couldn't get away from it, he had to ask whoever had got their hand up. What we were asking were all relevant questions, honest questions, and they deserved an honest answer but there were no honest answers. Everybody was condemning him for what he was trying to do in Leicestershire. In the end – he'd sussed us obviously – and he said, 'Look, I'm doing what I believe in. The Dirty Thirty did what they believed in and I admire them for it.' Well, that started everybody laughing. We were laughing ourselves. Everybody was laughing at Terry Hughes for saying he *admired the Dirty Thirty.'*

"That meeting, I believe, was the biggest factor in stopping the UDM coming into Leicestershire. Later there was a ballot, and Jack Jones did probably the only decent thing he did in his life. Even though they offered him a high position in the UDM – he did stick with the NUM." Richo's opinion of Jack's decision to stay in the NUM was: "In the end, Jack Jones didn't go UDM, he stayed NUM. We'd frit him to death."

Mel's final comment on Terry Hughes was that although he argued that the UDM was a more democratic union than the NUM, he would not abide by the decision of the Leicestershire ballot. "They had their ballot, and obviously the UDM people weren't going to abide by a ballot to stay NUM. Do you think Terry Hughes abided by the ballot? No, he'd already joined the UDM by then. He didn't want a ballot. In the UDM, a ballot's fine but not one that doesn't go for you. He turned out to be what we always knew he was. Amazingly he's now living in South Yorkshire, in Barnsley! Living in South Yorkshire, he'll have to watch whatever he says. I wouldn't like to live like that, having to watch your every word."

# Conclusion

It is now twenty-five years since the strike began. The Dirty Thirty have gone their different ways. Some have retired through either their age or, as in the case of Richo, because of ill health. One, Darren Moore, took a degree and now runs a benefit agency for Leicester City Council, and Sam Girvan teaches building skills at Coalville Tech. Mel Elcock works in engineering at the Brush in Loughborough, Mick Barnes is a tree surgeon, and several of the others are

*Cliff Jeffery (Geek) 2007.*

lorry or van drivers. Dave Douglas works for a firm of civil engineers, Phil Smith works as a handyman at an old folks' home. Cliff Jeffery lives in Anglesey, John Chiswell in Blackpool. Andrew Warren emigrated to New Zealand, and Mark Findell to Spain.

All of them look back with pride at their action in 1984-85. Mel Elcock commented, "I am proud of what I did in the strike, I am proud of my family and our supporters. A lot of people come into this world, and they go, and that's all you can say about them: they came and they went. But my family had a history of fighting the enemies of the country in wartime, and fighting the enemies of the union – whether that meant the government of the day or whoever – in peacetime. That's a family history that I'm proud of.

*A Dirty Thirty reunion in 2007.*

I've got friends from one end of the country to the other now, who I can visit at any time. I've got a welcome all over the country, and they've got a welcome here. The Dirty Thirty are my lifelong friends. We don't see each other every week, or every month or every year. It wouldn't matter if we didn't see each other for ten years. When we had our twenty-year reunion, I hadn't seen some of the lads more than once or twice in the whole of that twenty years. Then we got together it was like we were back there. Although we don't see each other very often, I do know that if ever I was in any trouble, I've got twenty-nine people I could turn to, knowing full well I would get whatever support I needed.

"Now we're coming up to our twenty-fifth anniversary and we will be having a get-together and a celebration of our struggle. I don't feel like a hero or anything, but for us to stand up to be counted against two and a half thousand men in Leicestershire, is an indictment on my county – and I'm Leicestershire born and bred. Just a few men stood up to be counted."

Wag Burton agrees. "I'd do it again, thinking of my family and my job. Looking back we were doing the right thing. I'll always stick by it. I'd do it again – with them lads anyway. Them lads were brilliant, all of them. Fantastic they were. I never had no fallouts with none of them. They kept us all going, Benny and Richo. They had the gift of the gab, but I ain't got that. I'm good with my hands, I do my talking with them."

Phil Smith was less sure about doing it again, but he was certain that it was the right thing to do. "It was an experience I'll never ever forget, but I wouldn't want to go through it again. I am glad I did it though. Today you're not going to get them sort of strikes, because there's nothing left. That was the last hurrah if you like. Ever since that it's all gone downhill. Thatcher picked on the biggest union, thinking if she could take the strongest out, everything else would collapse. They sold everything off. Now we're reaping the 'benefits' of Thatcherism. This is what she wanted, and New Labour has adopted her ways. It doesn't matter who you vote for today, you get the same thing."

Dave Douglas said, "It was the right thing to do, without a doubt. I'd do it again. To tell you the truth, when we went back to the pit, there were no bands playing, there were no banners, like in Wales. There was nothing. Our hearts were low but we went back with our heads held high."

Malcolm Pinnegar concluded, "I've always stood up for what I believed was fair and protested against exploitation, victimisation and bullying. I'd worked with and represented some excellent steadfast men in industrial disputes before going to work at the pit. So you can imagine my absolute disappointment that so many miners in my own county, members of the NUM – considered to be the vanguard of the trade union movement – should fall so short when called upon to support the fight to save their own and industry and their trade union rights. All excuses by these men and their local leaders are lamentable. The miners that blacklegged during the strike were the single biggest reason that the strike became unwinnable. Far too many of the NUM's resources of manpower, time and finances were spent with the objectives of making the strike 100%. This was completely understandable but it became a bridge too far. I'm sure that the Dirty Thirty, with their resolve and experience from twelve months on strike, were instrumental in making sure that Leicestershire did not follow Notts into the UDM.

*Malcolm Pinnegar (Benny), still spreading the word in 2007.*

"Now, a quarter of a century on, three-quarters of the coal used in Britain comes from abroad. Private contractors apply for and receive permission from the government to open cast mine on greenfield sites all over Britain, promising massive cuts in carbon emissions but leaving experimentation on clean burn coal technology mainly to other countries.

"The striking miners and their supporters have every right to say *we told you so*, as many of their predictions have come true. The consequences of the miners losing the 1984-85 strike have had a detrimental effect on many working people, their rights, their communities and their way of living. The strike for us wasn't about money, it was about loyalties, values and rights. Today, lots of people believe there are no discernable differences between the political parties, and the gap between rich and poor has never been greater. Wage increases are only ever made in percentage terms. 5% of a lot is a big pay rise; 5% of eff-all is eff-all. Many people work longer hours than their forebears did in the 1920s. People are in more debt than ever before, but have been encouraged to live beyond their means. Thatcher's 'I'm-all-right-Jack' philosophy still abounds in England, and she has even been celebrated in Downing Street by a Labour Prime Minister. Money is the god, and avarice has replaced respect. So in conclusion, Thatcher and her blacklegs have got their way for the past twenty-five years, but I'm sure, as we are seeing at the present and will see in the future, people will come to see that we were right all along.

"Ironically, Thatcher and her lackeys made possible one of the most enduring experiences of my life: receiving help from people we never met, and meeting people from all part of the UK and different countries of the wider world. It reminds us that there are like-minded people everywhere. Thatcher called them her 'enemies within', but to me they are my heroes within and without. I will never forget them. I thought long and hard about making a contribution to this book, but I suppose my decision was inevitable. It was made not wishing to brag or to limelight, but wishing to acknowledge all striking miners from whichever coalfield they came and everyone who shared the journey through the miners' strike with the Dirty Thirty."

The Dirty Thirty were regarded with honour and respect in every coalfield in England, bar Leicestershire, although even here, there was some grudging respect. In the official history of the Leicestershire NUM, hardly a source of admiration for the Dirty Thirty, it is recorded, "Through their level of activity which was out of all proportion to their numbers, the Dirty Thirty came to have considerable symbolic significance." Dave Douglas commented, "Having a memorable name like the Dirty Thirty done us the

*Durham Gala 2008.*

*Margaret Pinnegar, Wendy Jeffery and Kay Smith at the Durham Gala 2008.*

world of good, and it still does to this day. If we had just been the Leicestershire Striking Miners, it wouldn't have had the impact. We became known."

Although none of the Dirty Thirty consider themselves as heroes, there are parts of the country where that is exactly how they are regarded. Several of the Thirty, with their families, attend the annual Miners' Gala in Durham, known as 'The Big Meeting'. In 2008, they were there with their banner, when they were approached by a bandsman from one of the colliery brass bands. Dave Douglas recalled with some understandable pride, "At the Durham Gala this year, I was standing with the banner and a bandsman came over in his uniform. He says, 'The Dirty Thirty! Are you all here?' I said, 'No, with our wives there's about ten of us.' He was from Sunderland, and he said to us, 'We'd be honoured to have you walk in front of our band with your banner. We'll be playing for you.' So as soon as band came level with where we were standing, a gap opened up because he stopped his band. We got in, and we marched with our banner held high and a band behind us, playing for the Dirty Thirty."

Can anyone doubt that the Dirty Thirty are rightly regarded as heroes of the miners' strike?

*The Dirty Thirty carry their banner with pride at the Durham Gala 2008.*